PUBLISHER N

Cataloging-in-Publication Data has been applied for and may be obtained from the Library of Congress.

ISBN: 978-1-947215-15-3

Book design by Joseph Stevenson
Cover design by Joseph Stevenson

Published in 2020 by Golden Valley Publishing, LLC.

Printed and bound in U.S.A.

Golden Valley Press books are available at special discounts when purchased in quantity for premiums and promotions as well as fundraising or educational use. Special editions can also be created to specification.

Golden Valley Press
PO BOX 531412
Henderson, NV 89052

HOW TO DRAW ANIME

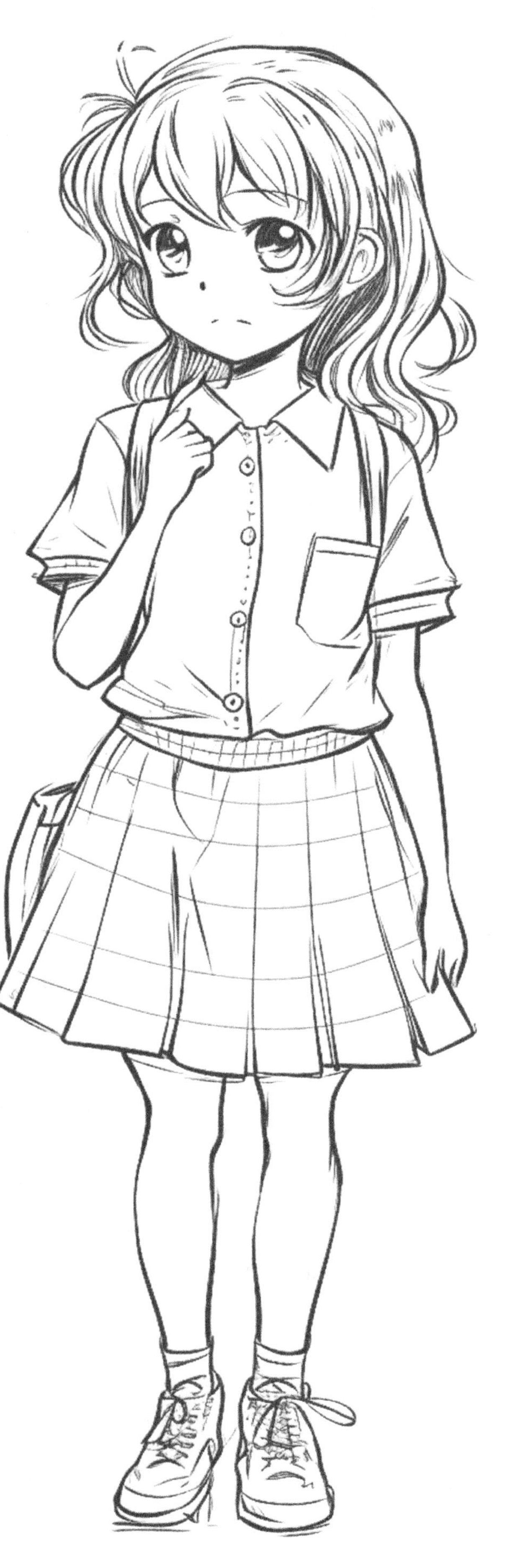

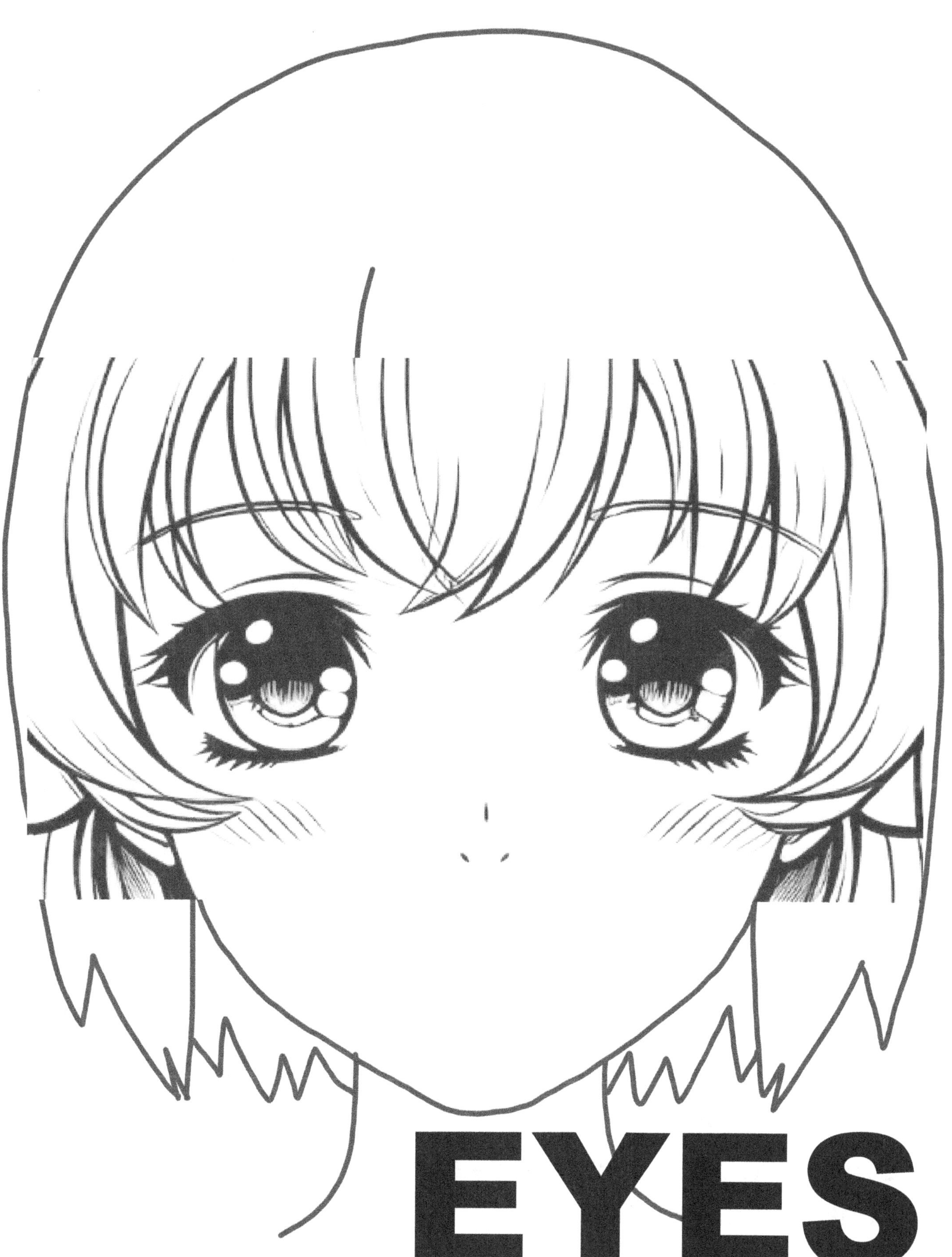
EYES

EYES

The eyes are at the center of Anime drawing and are arguably the hardest to master.

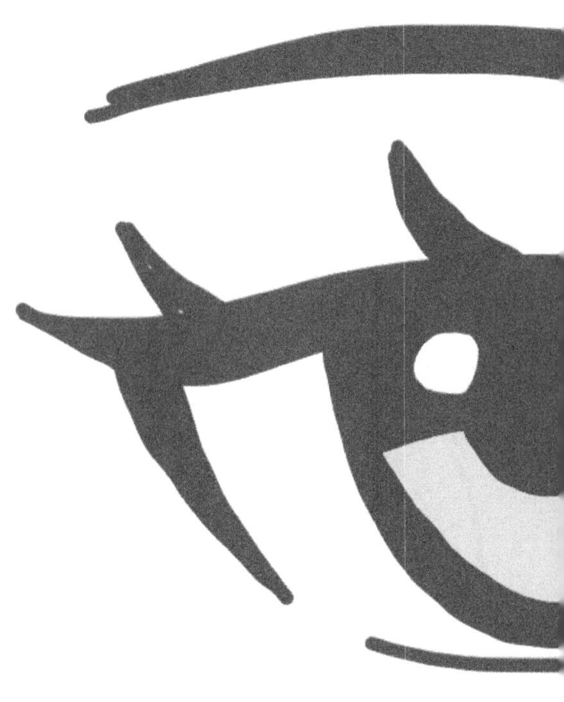

Drawing Anime characters will require a lot of discipline and practice.

The eyes are no exception and require a lot of time to master.

Eyes are what change the look of your anime character. Often you can have the hair, mouth and other features stay the same but change the eyes and your character will completely change.

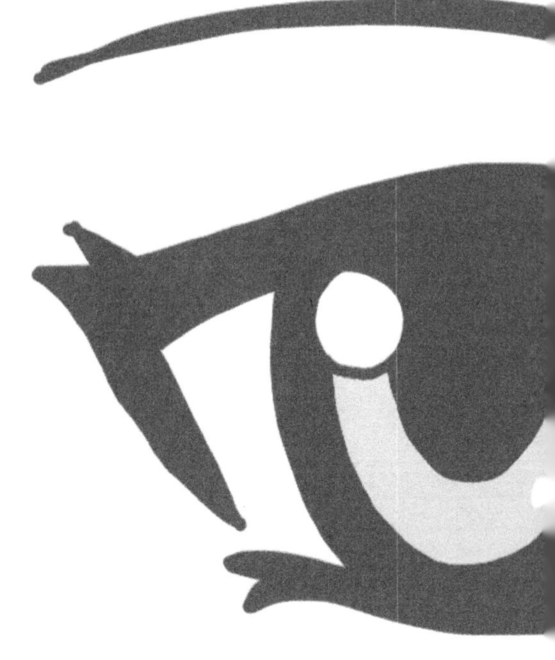

There are multiple styles of eyes, all of which we can't cover in just one book. We will cover though some of the more popular ones and give you the tools you need to start drawing your own eyes in no time at all. Let's get you started!

THREE TYPES OF EYES

In Anime drawings, there are three main styles of eyes. We will go into the details of each in the following pages. The eyes styles we are going to cover in this book are:

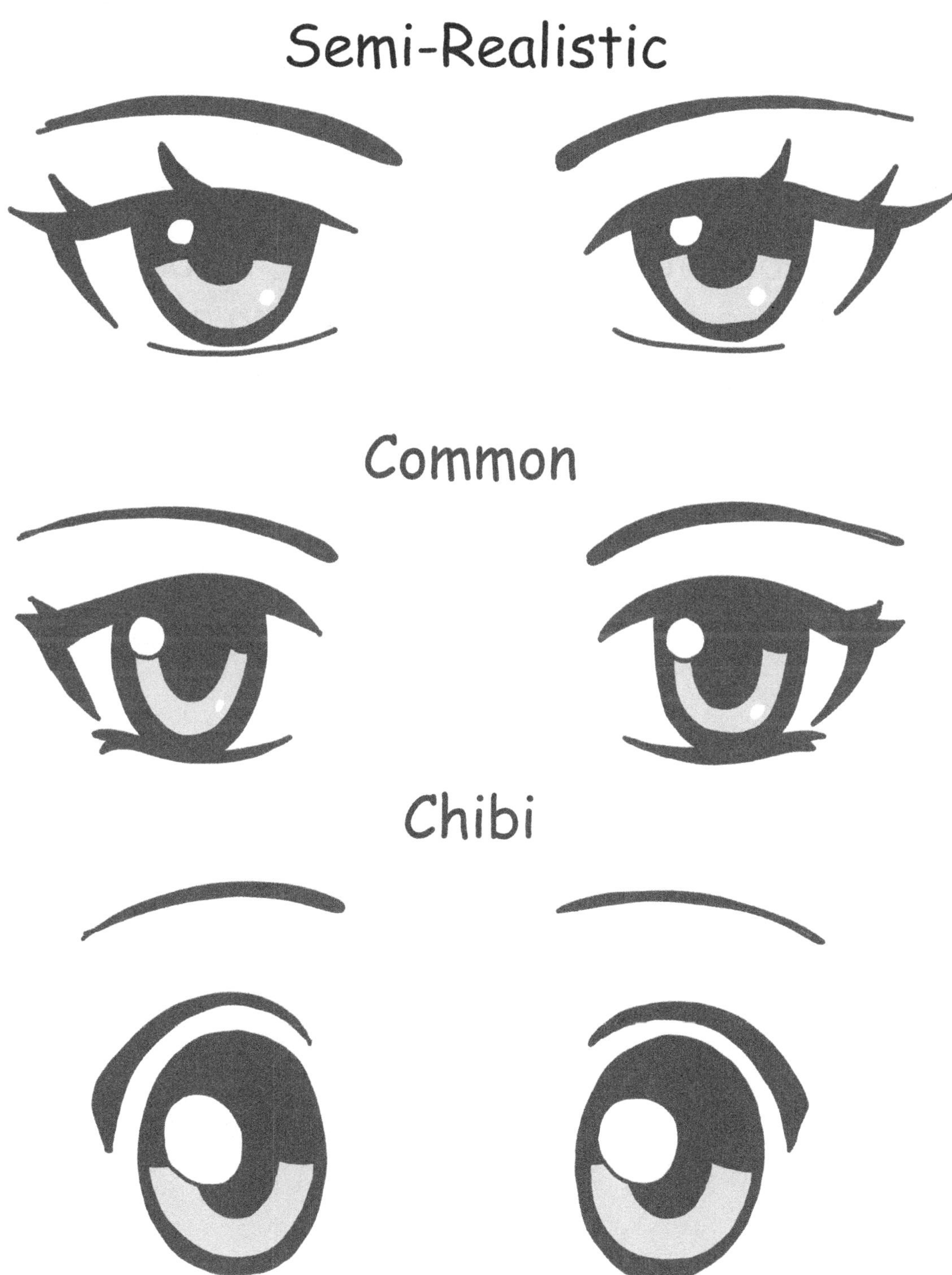

SEMI-REALISTIC

We will start with the most common eye type which is semi-realistic:

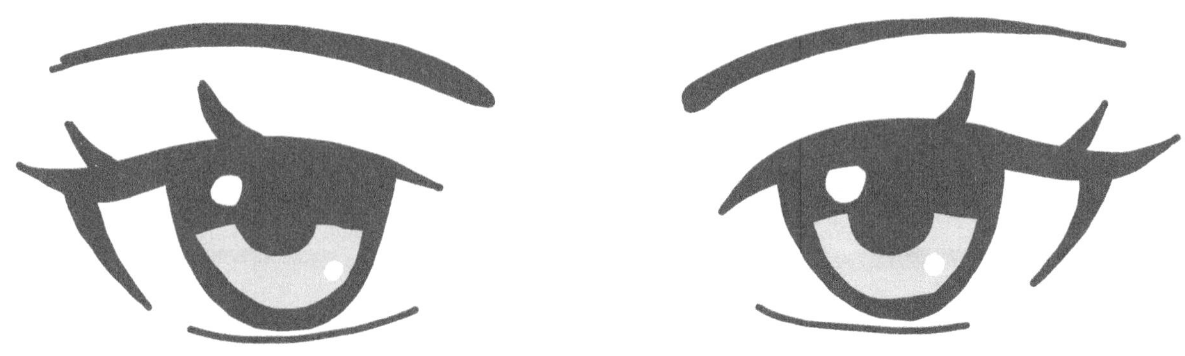

To start, begin with the eyelashes. For basic eyes it should look like two raindrops pointing at each other, the largest part of the drop pointing inwards. They do not have to be identical but should have similar lengths and heights.

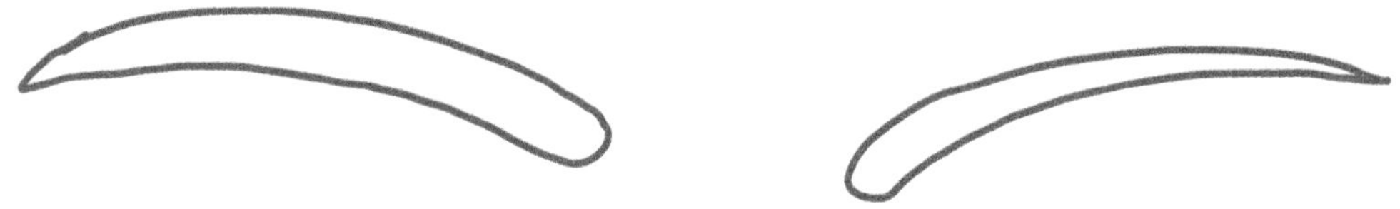

The height and width is a personal preference. As you practice you can adjust the brows to change emotions. When you have a shape you are satisfied with fill inthe eyebrows with your pen or drawing tool.

You can correct any shape problems here.

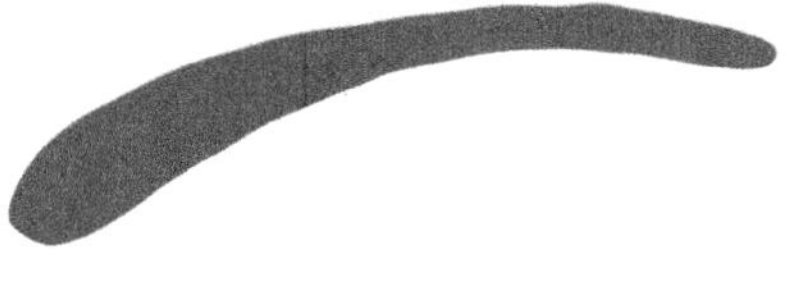

Once you have both eyebrows filled in, you can start on the eyelids. The eyelids follow the shape of the eyebrows in the middle but towards the ends they change direction and curve up.

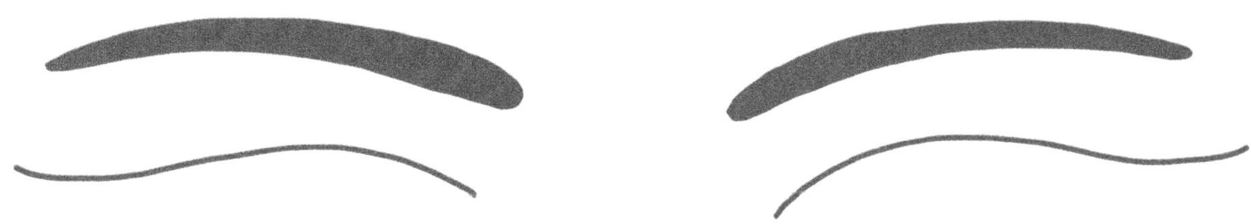

This shape will give you the top of the eye, but we need to make it thicker so that we can show the eye lashes.

Do this by adding in what look like shark fins along the top of the lines.

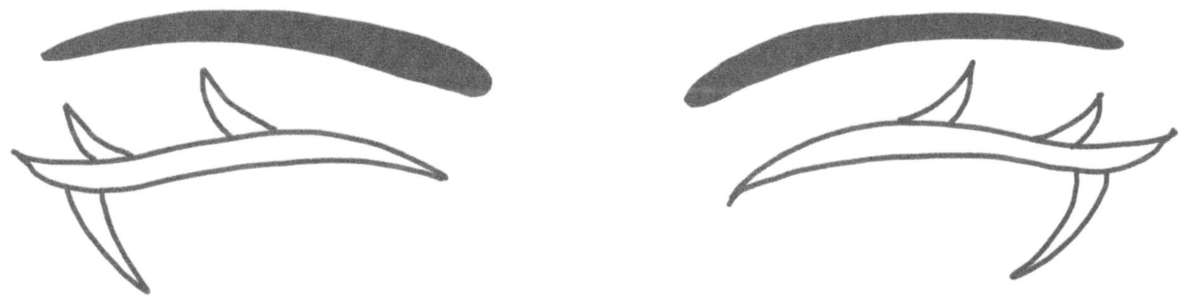

Add them to the sides of the eyes as well.

Pro-Tip: Practice makes perfect. Practice drawing wavy lines focusing on smooth lines. This will help when drawing eyes.

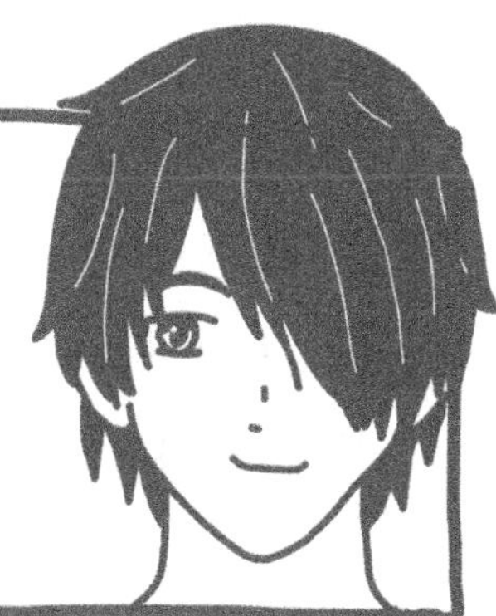

Now that you have all the fins drawn you can fill in the lashes and outline of the eye with your pen.

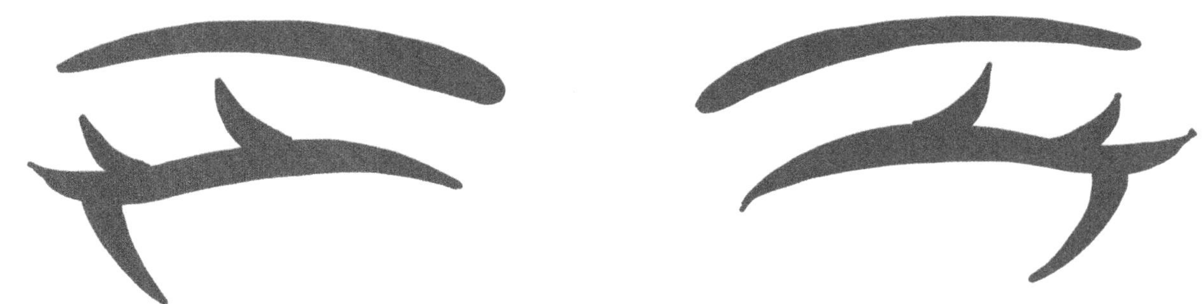

If your eyes don't look like the ones above try making smoother lines with your pen while you fill in the eyes.

If that still doesn't work, go back and try again. This portion of the eyes are the hardest. The shape of the eyes are determined at the beginning and can be very difficult to master. As you practice drawing smoother lines in directions you want, your hands will be able to hold the pen more steadily and your eyes will begin to look how you want them to.

Continue to practice drawing the eyelids and eyelashes until you are able to draw them without looking at the book or other pictures for reference.

You should be able to adjust the size, direction and overall look of the eyes based on how you want them shaped in your head vs. what you see from another drawing in front of you.

Practice Makes Perfect! Use the page below to practice drawing what you have learned so far.

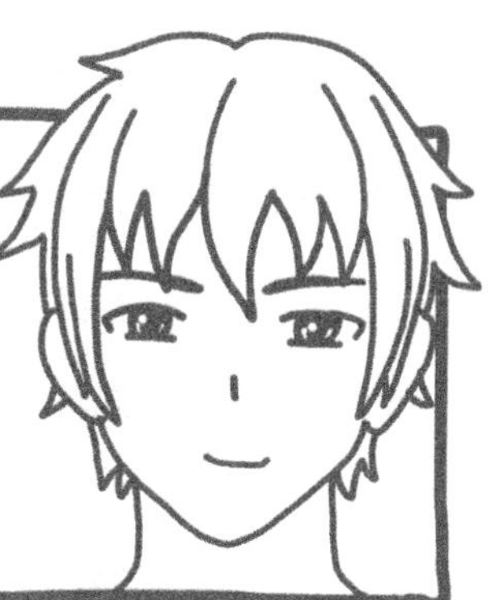

Next draw the bottom of the eyelid. This can be just a small curved line. It should make the shape of the eye.

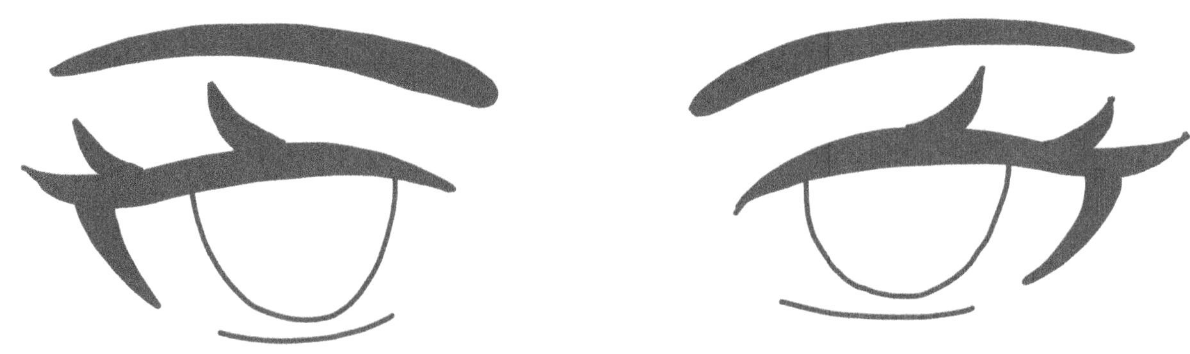

Once this is drawn add two half circles which will make up the pupil. The half circles should be centered. Now add two smaller circles in the eyes as shown. These are going to be the reflected light in the eyes.

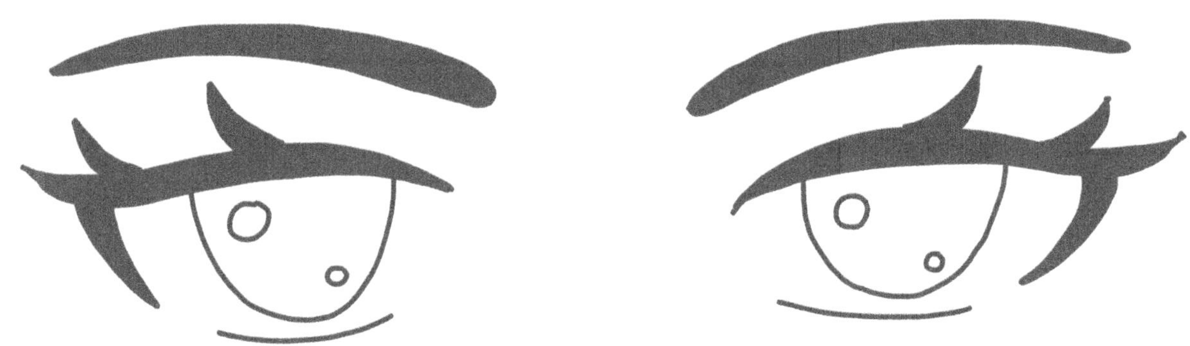

Add one "U" shape to the bottom of each eye.

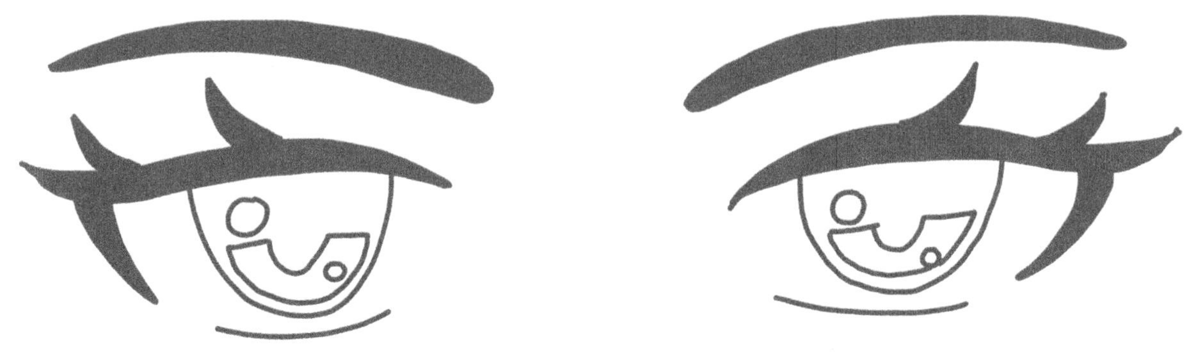

Finish the eyes by filling in the eye all exepct the small circles for light reflections and the "U" shape at the bottom of the eyes.

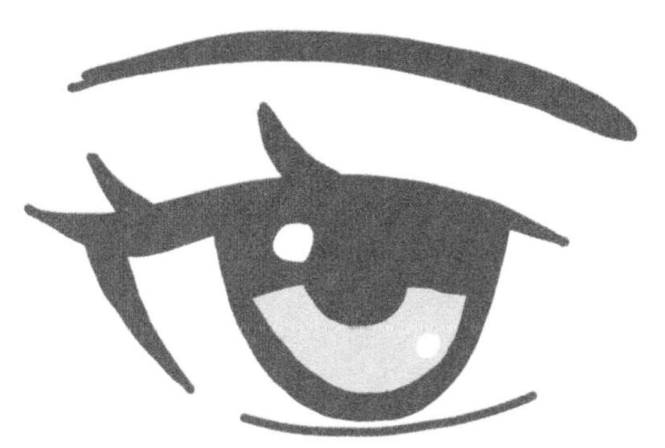
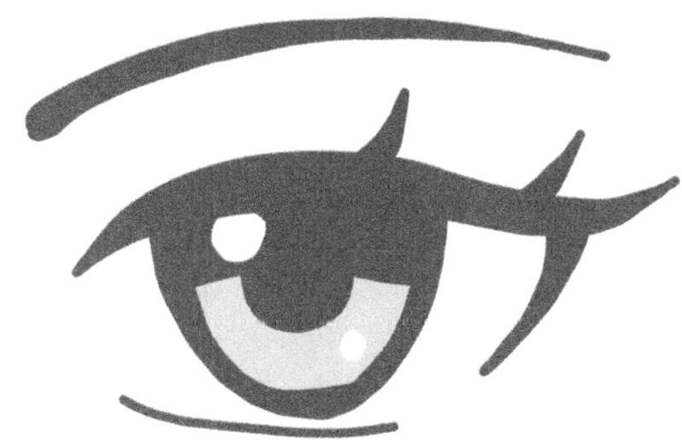

Fill in the "U" shapes with grey or if you are using color any color you would want the eyes to be.

Make sure you don't fill in the second light reflection but instead color around it.

If you are using a pen which is recommended for drawing Anime, try using a pencil to lightly color in the pupil area of the eye.

Practice drawing the eyes from memory, changing up shapes and adding in your own creativity.

Pro-Tip: Try waiting to draw the second light circle until you use the pupil color to avoid a dark line in the "U" shape.

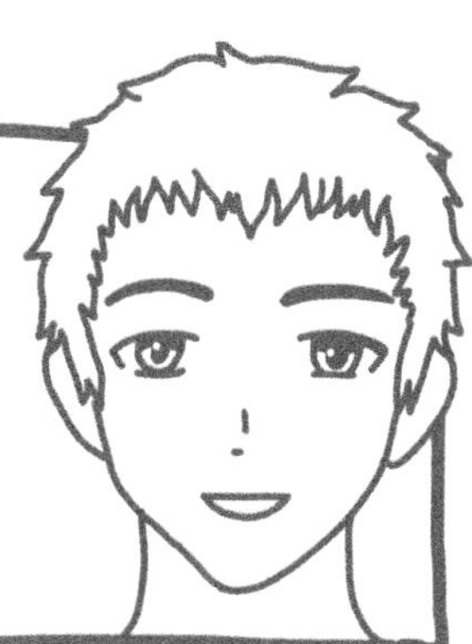

Practice Makes Perfect! Use the page below to practice drawing what you have learned so far.

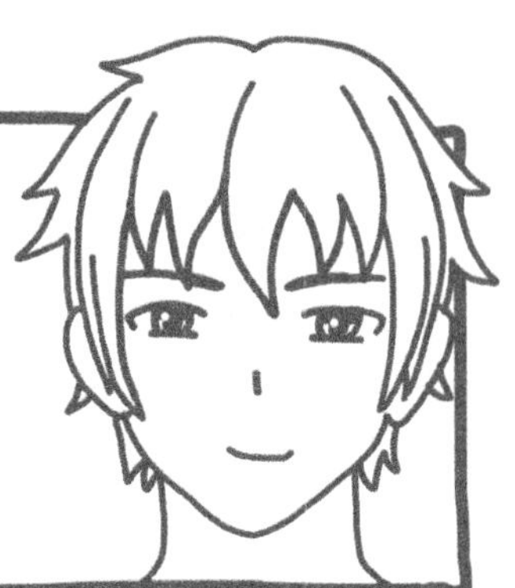

COMMON

The next type of eye that we will cover is the Common eye:

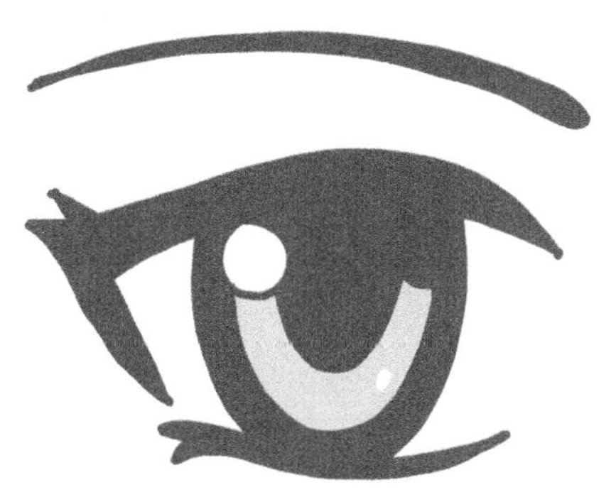

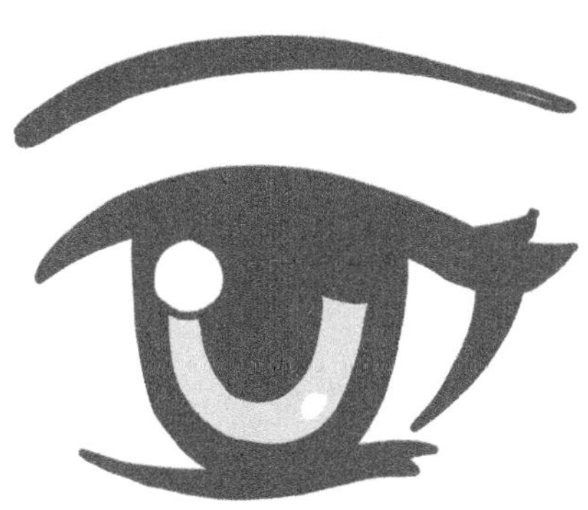

Common eyes are so named because they essentially are the most common style of eyes. The steps are very similar to the semi-realistic eye drawing steps.

There are a few differences between the two that should be noted:

1. Common eyes don't have all the fins at the top of the eyelashes.

2. Common eyes have thicker bottoms of the eyes vs. just a line on the semi-realistic eyes.

The eyebrows however are drawn the same way.

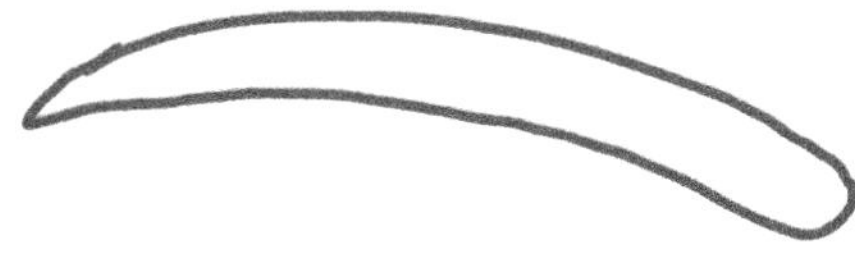

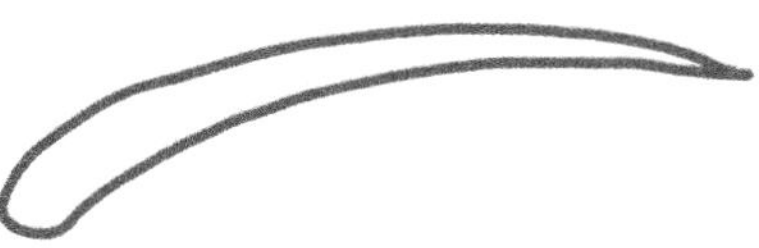

Keep the eyebrows and upper eyelids uniform to each other instead of opposite.

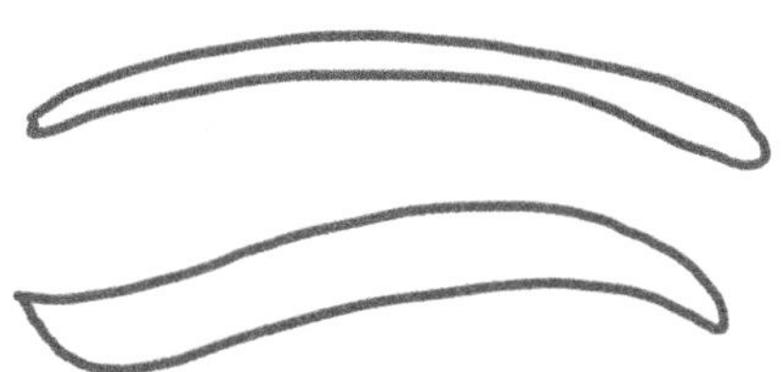 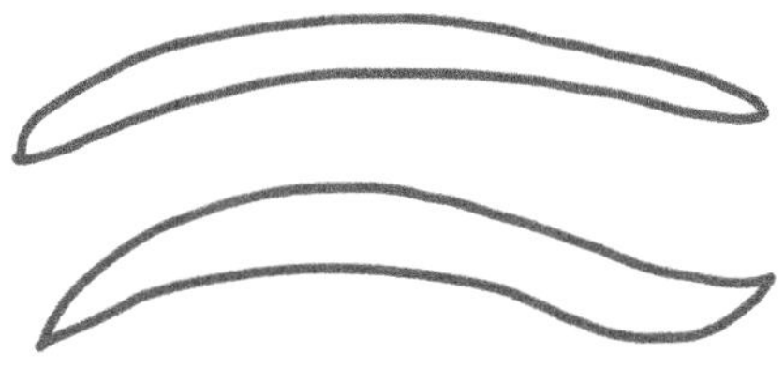

The eyelashes will generally follow the same rules as with semi-realistic. On each one though you will still add one fin on the top of the eye lash, and one to the side of the eye which will outline the eyeball like before.

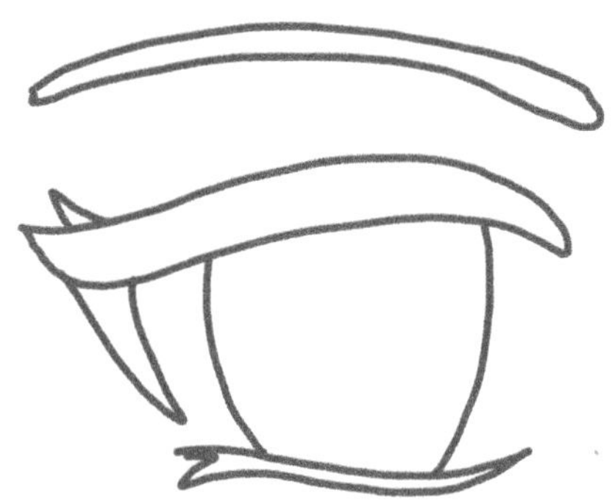 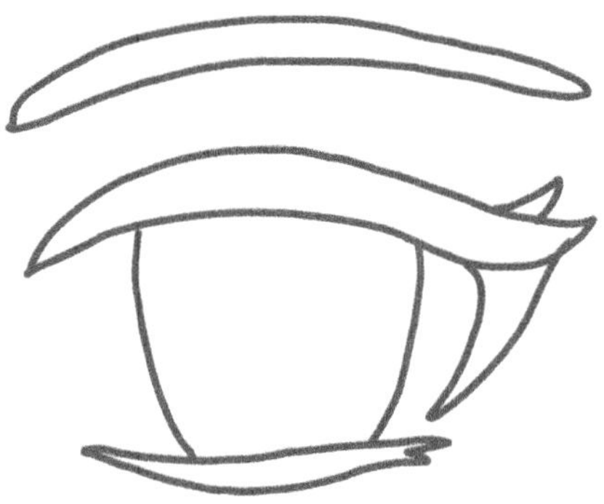

Add in the eyeballs last with semi-circles that fill from the center of the eye.

Pro-Tip: Practice drawing shapes over and over. This will make drawing the shapes in eyes much easier and more rote.

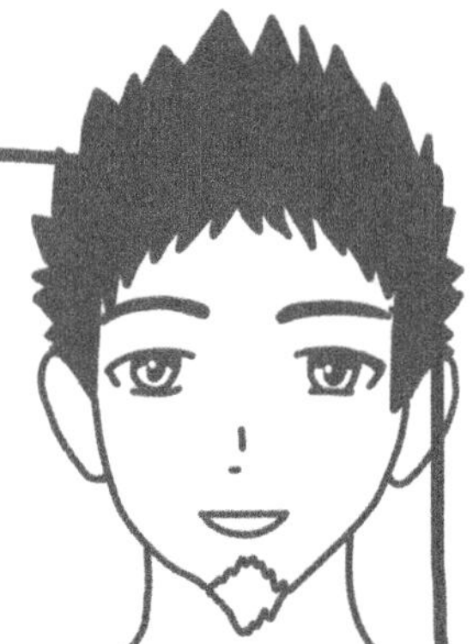

Practice Makes Perfect! Use the page below to practice drawing what you have learned so far.

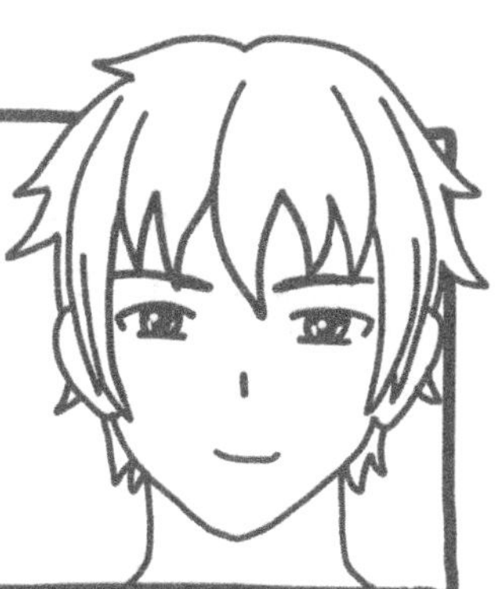

Before moving on, fill in the drawing with your pen except for the pupil area.

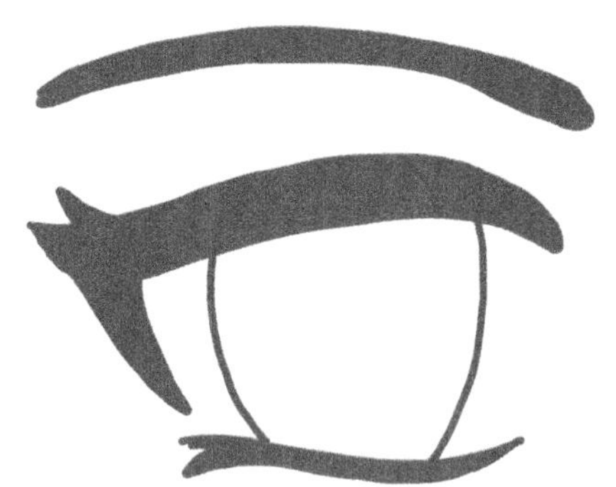
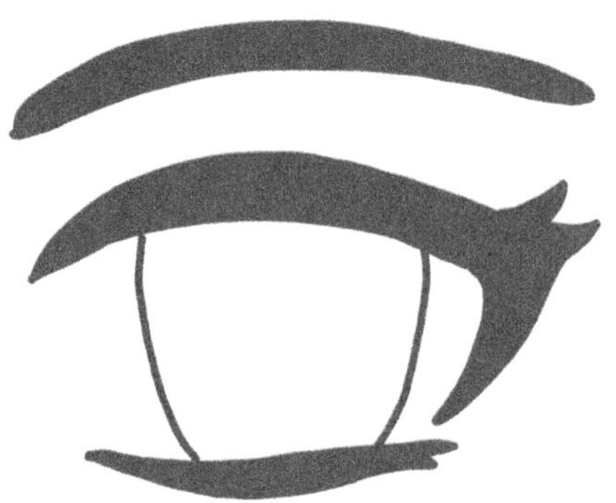

Now draw two circles again for the reflection of light that will be in the eyes. Add in a "U" shape to the bottom half of the pupils in the eye.

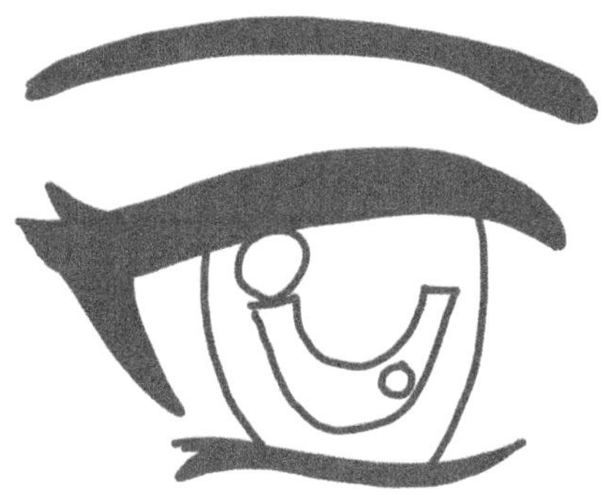
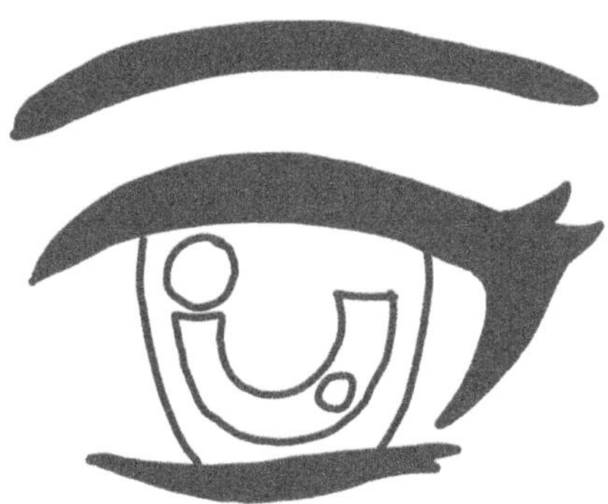

Finish with filling the pupils dark and the "U" shape with eye color or just grey.

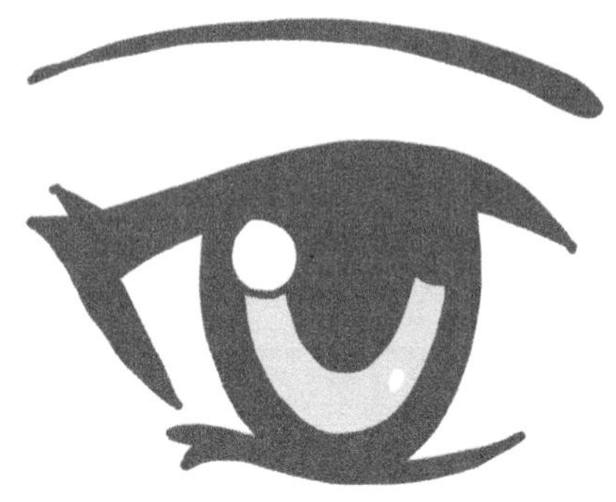
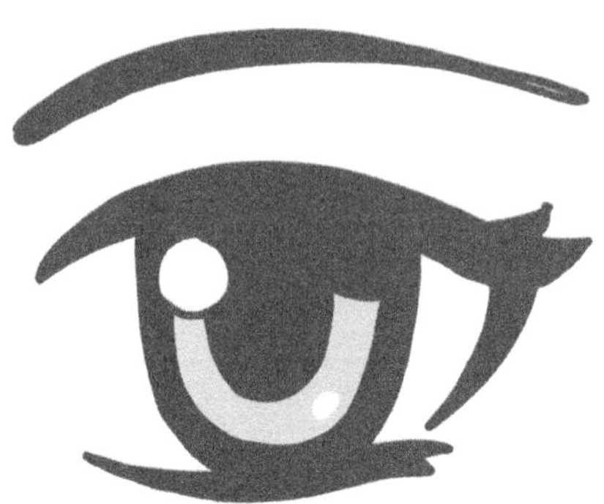

When you compare both finished types of eyes you will see a lot of similarities between them.

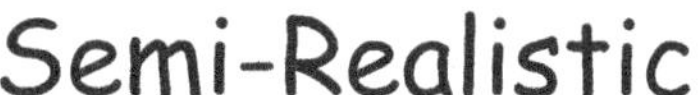

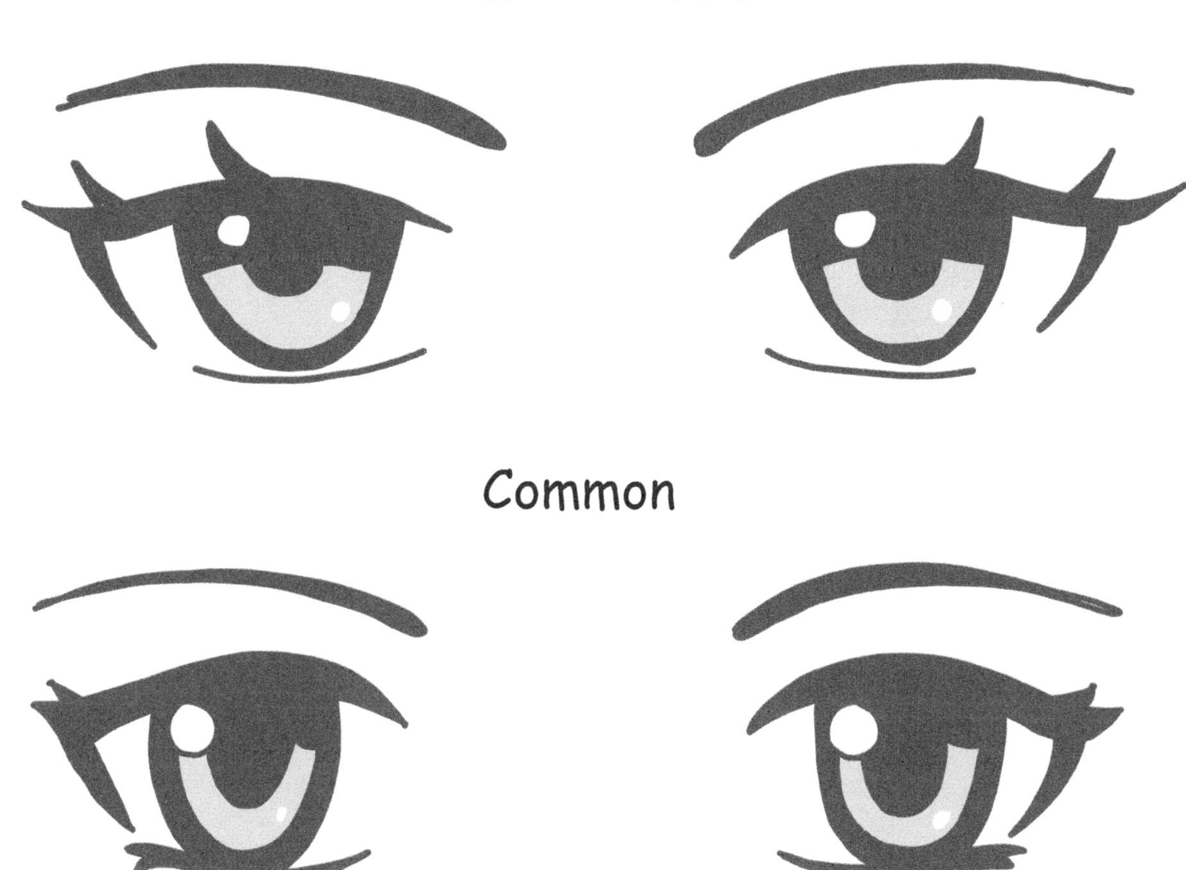

Both have reflections in their pupils, both have "U" shapes towards the bottom of the pupil, both have lashes, eyebrows and eyelids.

The biggest difference between the two is that semi-realistic eyes have more details in them than common eyes do. There are more lashes, points, curves etc.

Now its time to move on to the last eye-type.

Practice Makes Perfect! Use the page below to practice drawing what you have learned so far.

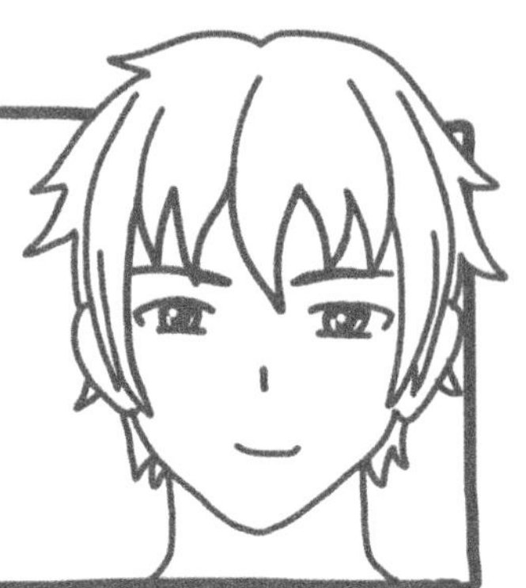

CHIBI

The last type of eyes we will cover are called "Chibi":

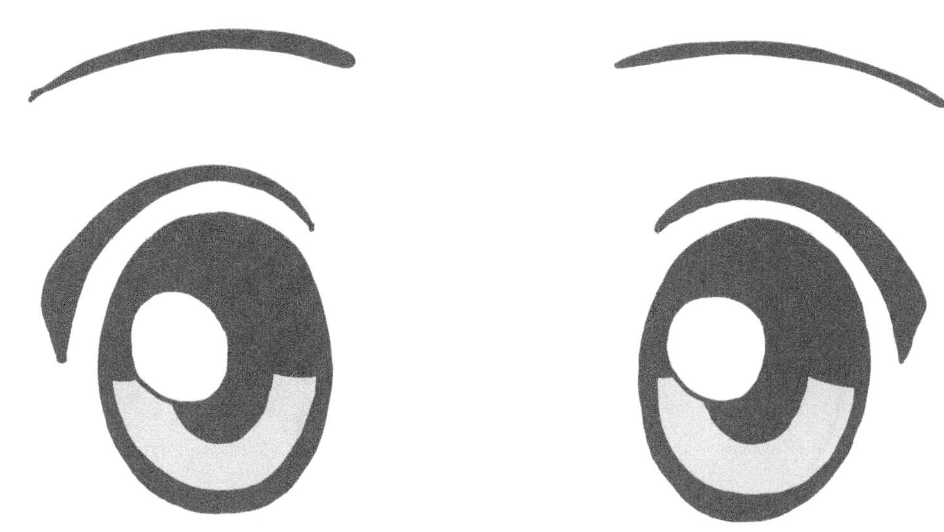

Chibi is a type of anime that features large heads and large eyes.

Usually the characters have smaller bodies so they look more cartoonish and less realistic.

To draw chibi eyes you will use the same steps but with a few variations and more rounded shapes.

Pro-Tip: Chibi has a lot less detail than other anime. Focus on rounded shapes to make your cute chibi look great!

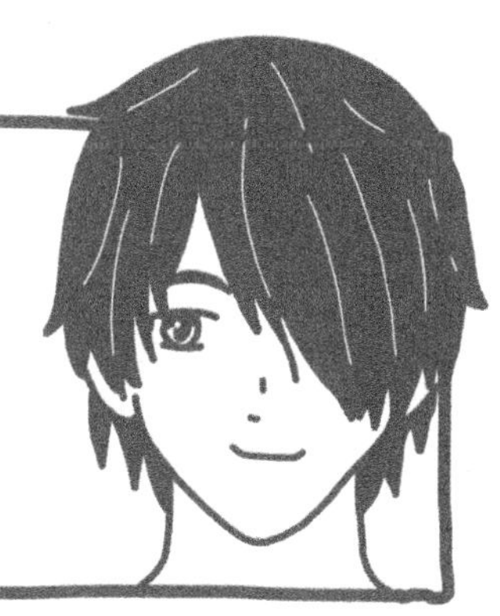

Like the other eyes, start with the eyebrows. They will be shaped just like the others as two rain-drops that are pointed towards each other.

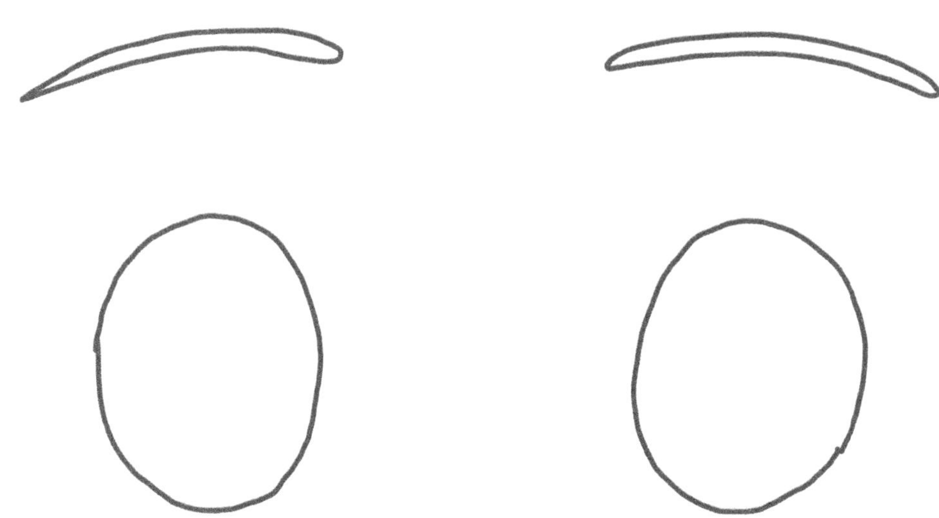

Unlike the other eyes however you will start by drawing two ovals below the brows. Add once circle for the light reflection and then a "U" shape behind that circle on the bottom half of the circle. Chibi eyes have less steps than the other two styles.

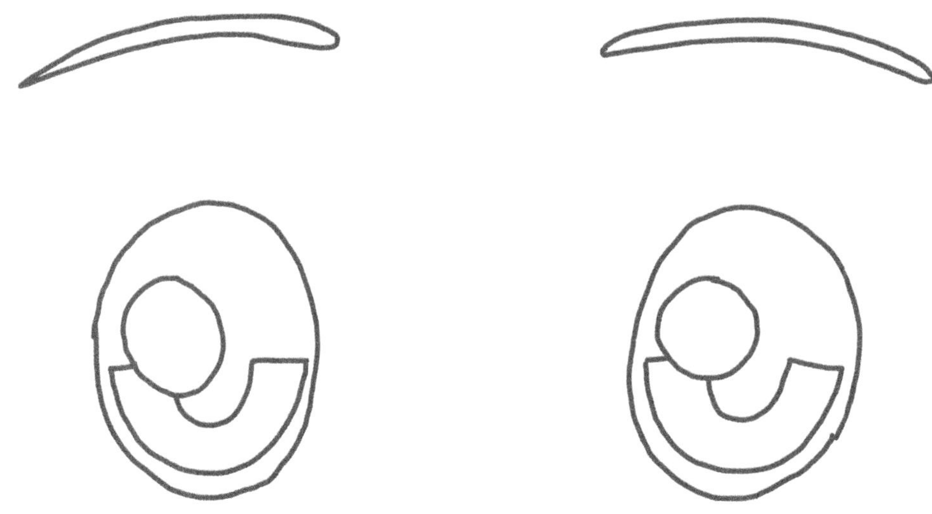

Practice Makes Perfect! Use the page below to practice drawing what you have learned so far.

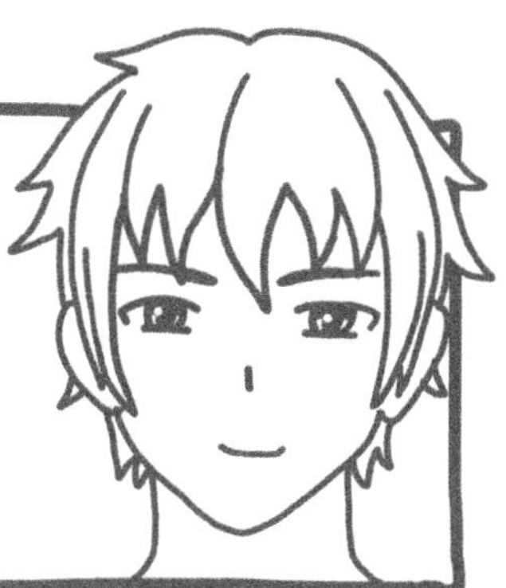

Now fill in the eyes with black and the pupils with the eye color you would like. You can also use grey with Chibi.

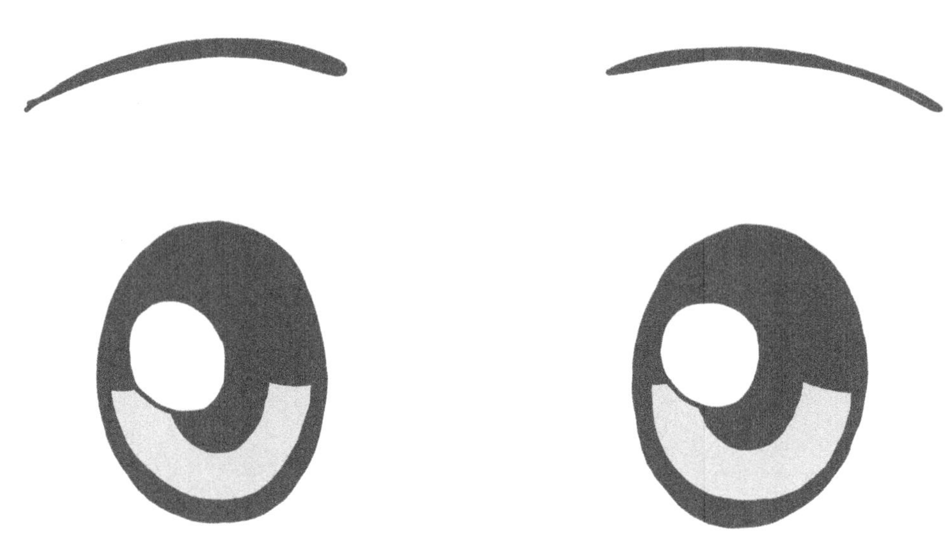

You can end here if you like but adding lashes will allow you to change the emotion of your chibi much easier. Add lashes by drawing a swoosh shape above each eyeball. One end should be pointy with the other one wider that is on the edge of the eye.

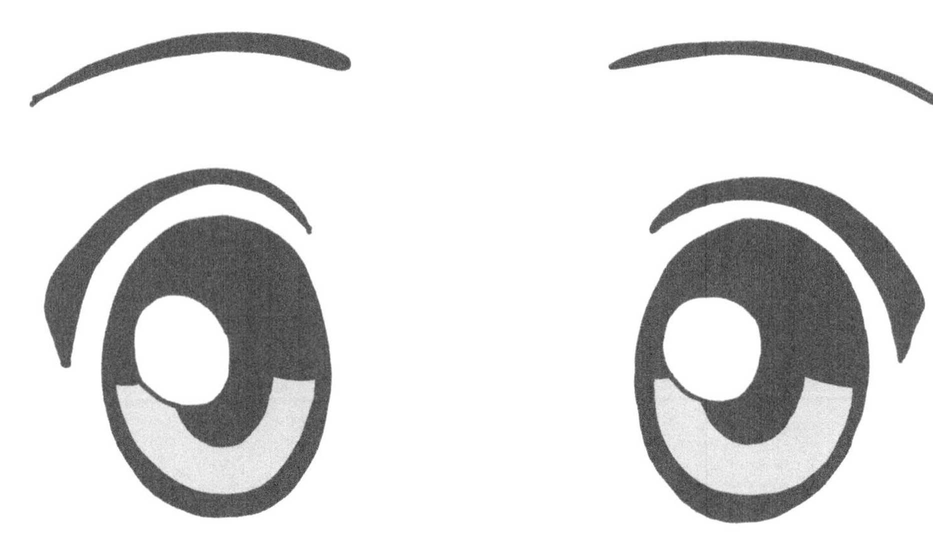

Practice Makes Perfect! Use the page below to practice drawing what you have learned so far.

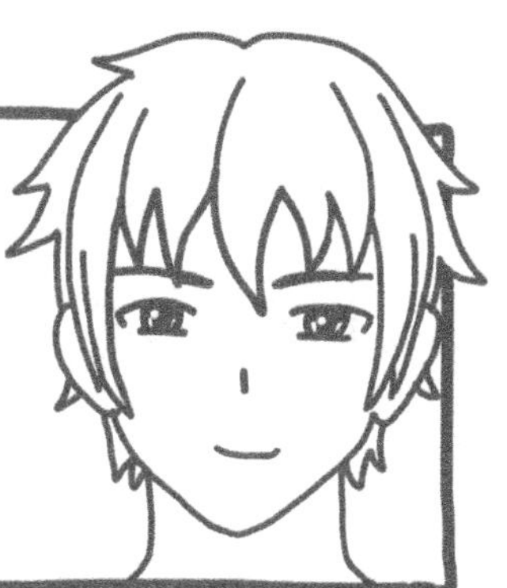

You should now be able to draw three of the most popular types of anime eyes:

Semi-Realistic

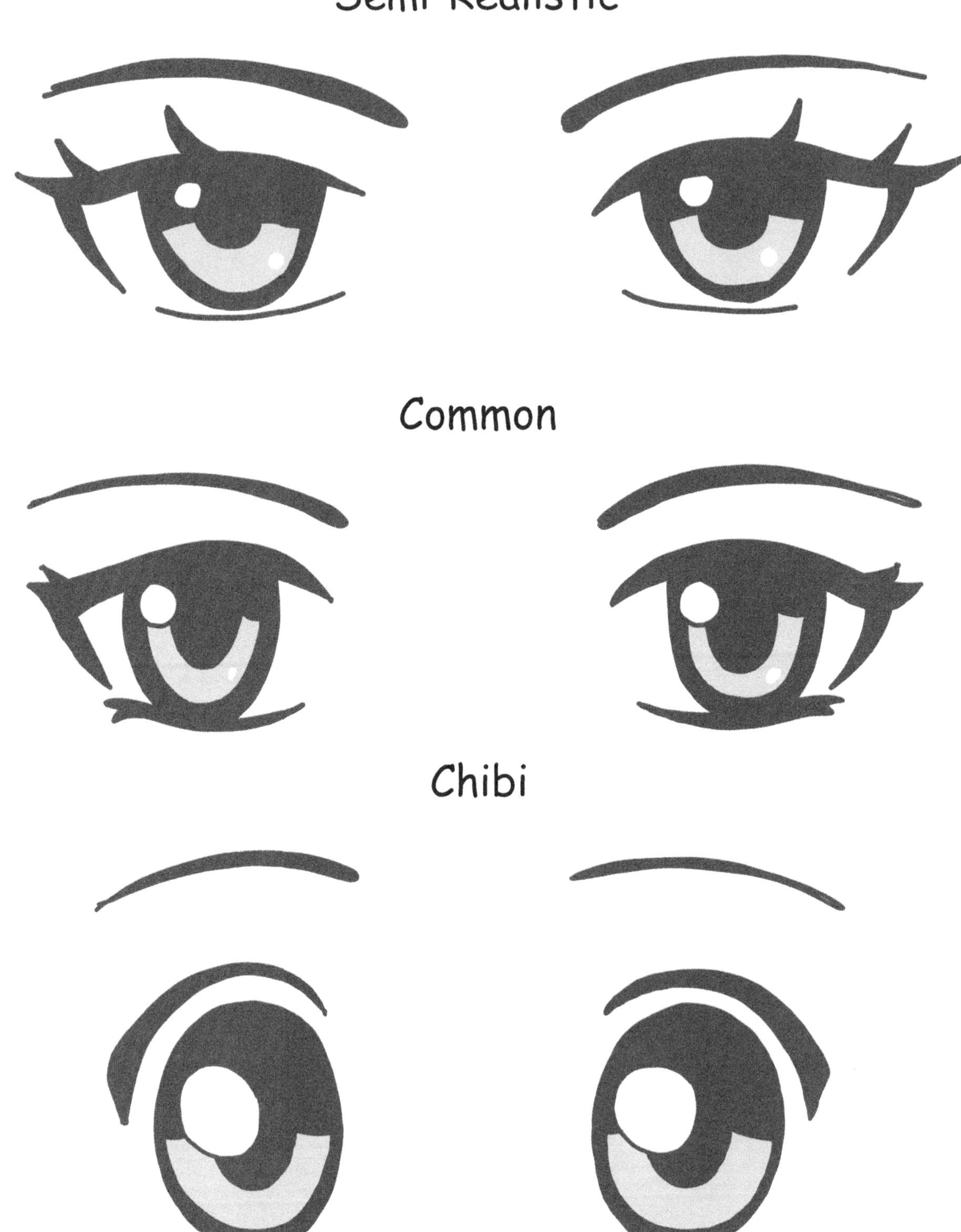

Up to this point we have covered eyes looking straight. As you learn to change angles of the head and proportions, the steps for drawing the eyes will remain the same.

The shapes however will change to match the direction the eyes are looking. Here are some examples.

Looking Straight

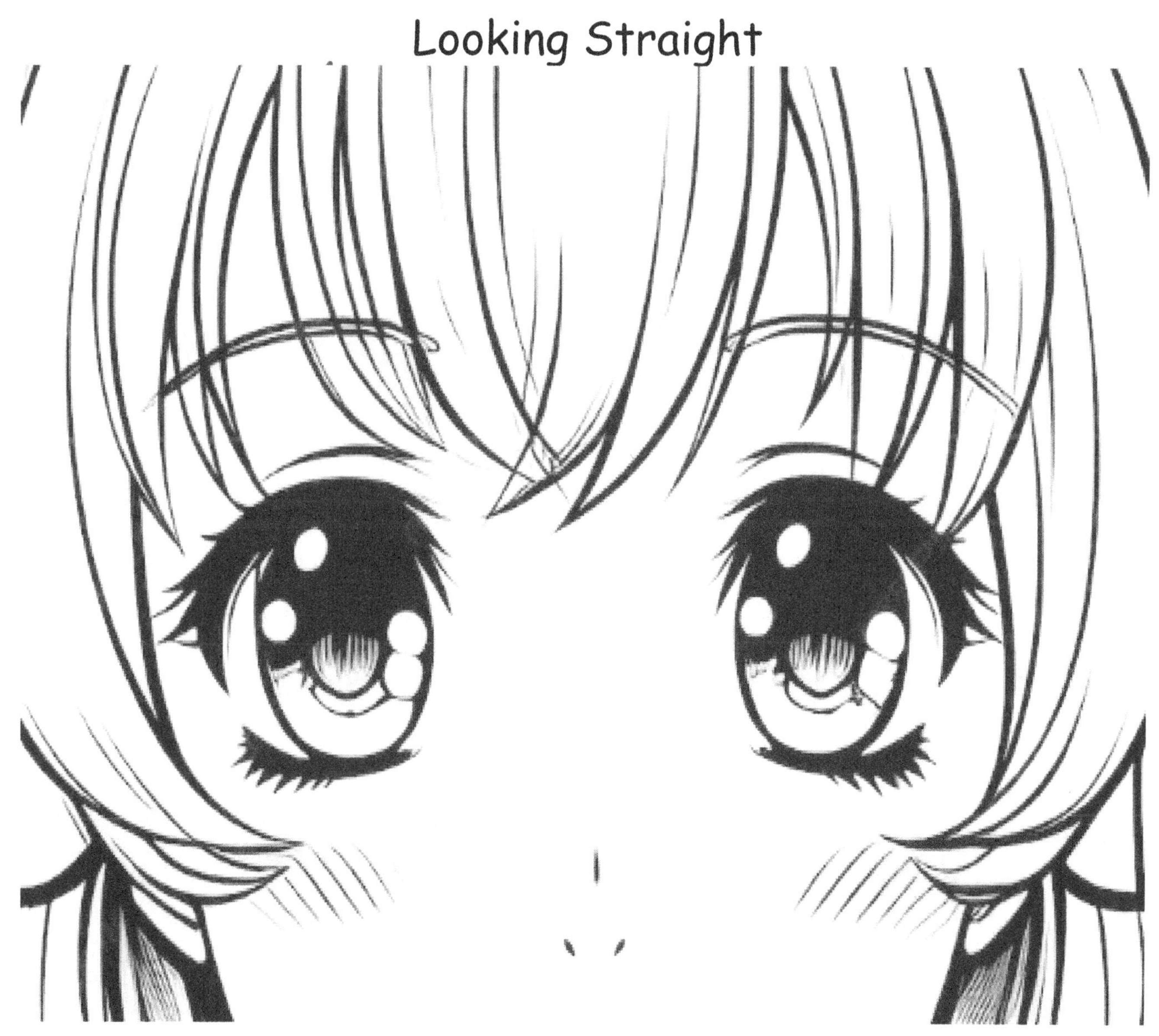

Looking to the Side

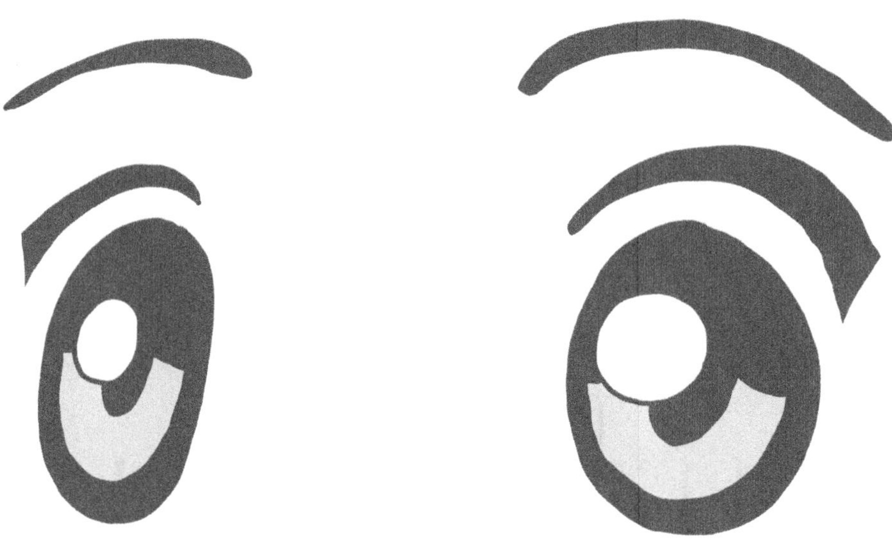

The steps are the same, but to have your character look to the left, make one eye smaller and more narrow than the other.

Do the opposite if you want your eyes to look the other way. To make the eyes look further in one direction, exagerate the sizes and changes you make.

Pro-Tip: Use pictures or other drawings to find examples of the size changes to eyes as directions change.

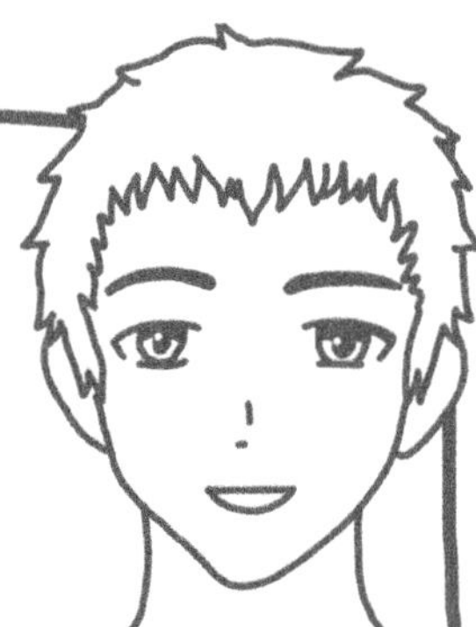

Looking Up

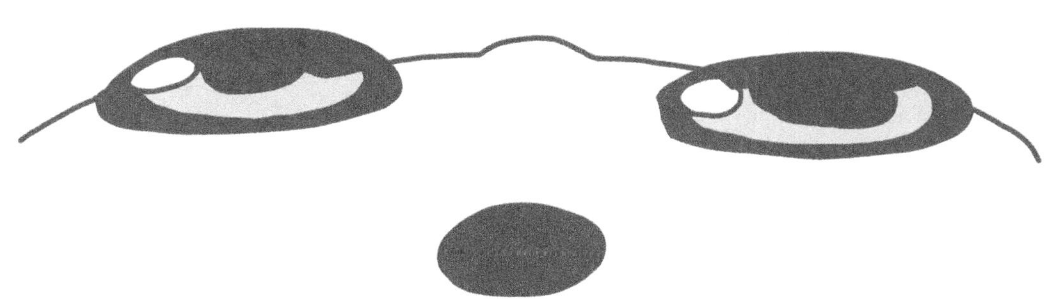

Instead of having vertical shaped eyes changing width which will change the direction of the eyes from side to side, lets try having the eyes look up.

To do this instead of making them not as wide you make the eyes not as tall.

Notice though that all of the shapes in the eye have to be adjusted. The light shape, the "U" shape, and the pupil itself all have to be changed to be more of an oval shape in order to make it look like the head is looking up.

You can actually use the exact same eyes to have your chibi character look down.

Use the same principles to determine what direction your character is looking.

Practice Makes Perfect! Use the page below to practice drawing what you have learned so far.

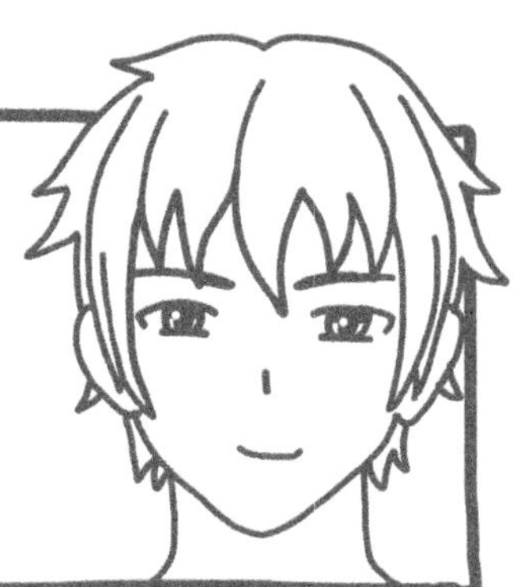

CONCLUSION

Eyes are again one of the harder parts of the body to draw in anime. From the details in the eyes themselves to the shape of the eyes or direction they are looking, mastering eyes will take a lot of practice.

As you go through the rest of this book, make sure you come back and occasionally practice drawing the eyes.

You will notice that as you master drawing the eyes you will get better at drawing other areas as well.

Don't get discouraged as you continue to learn to draw anime. Most artists take years to master their drawings.

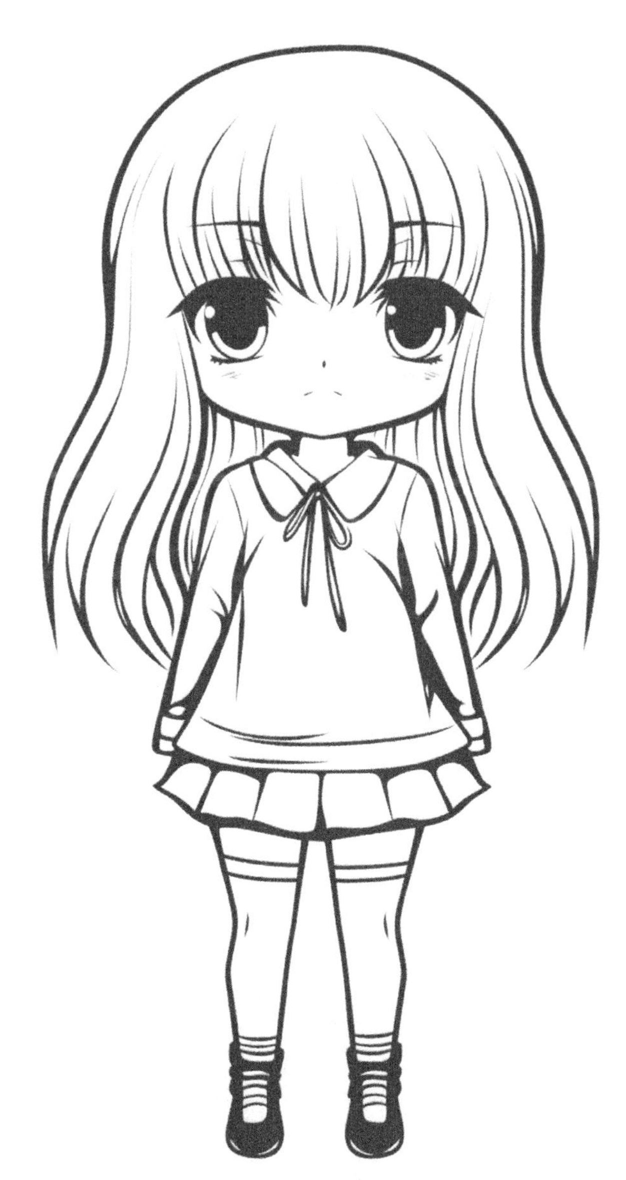

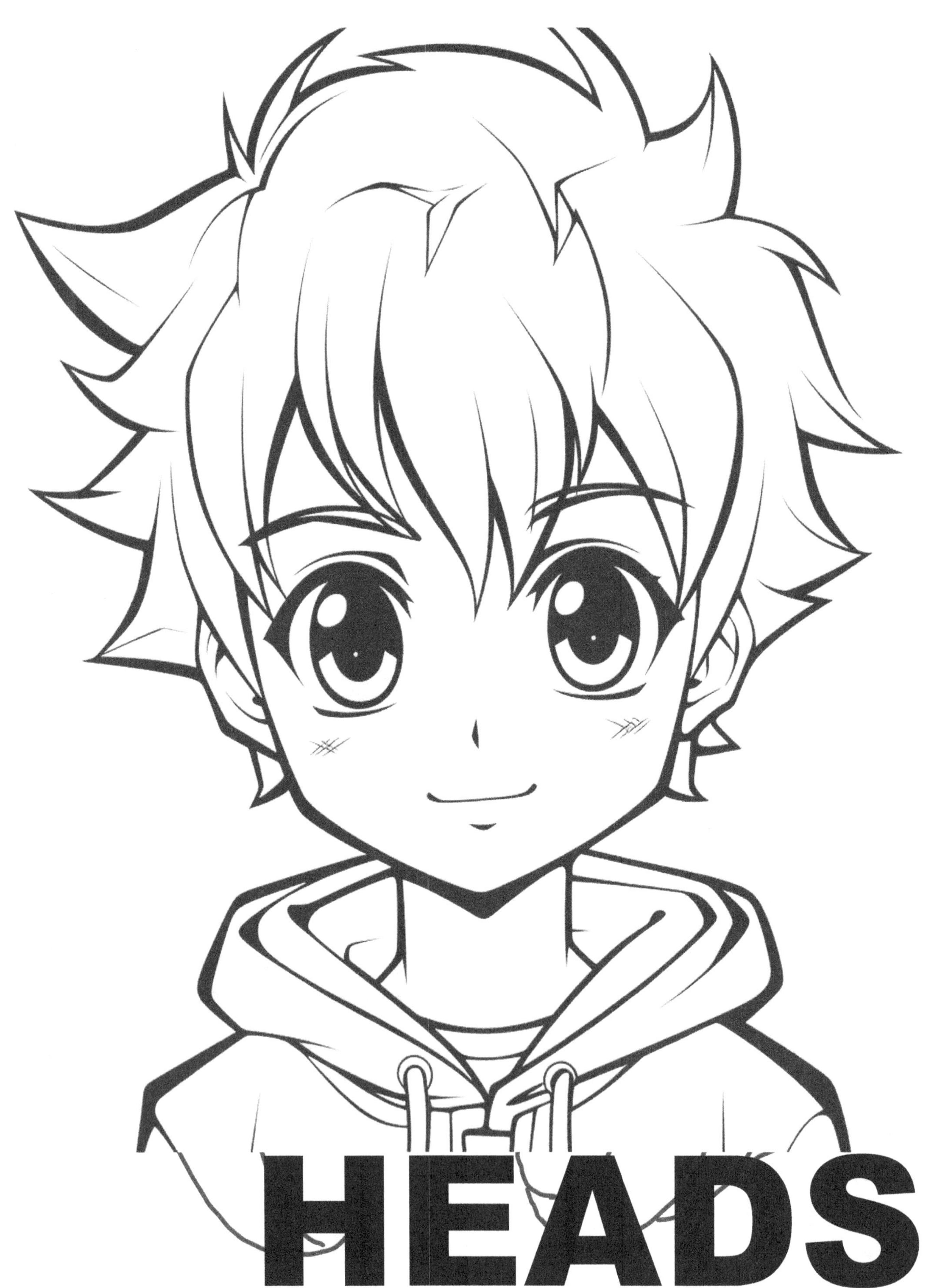
HEADS

HEADS

In anime drawing, heads are the main shape that contain the rest of the detail of the face. Most heads are the shape of an oval or circle, depending on the height of the character.

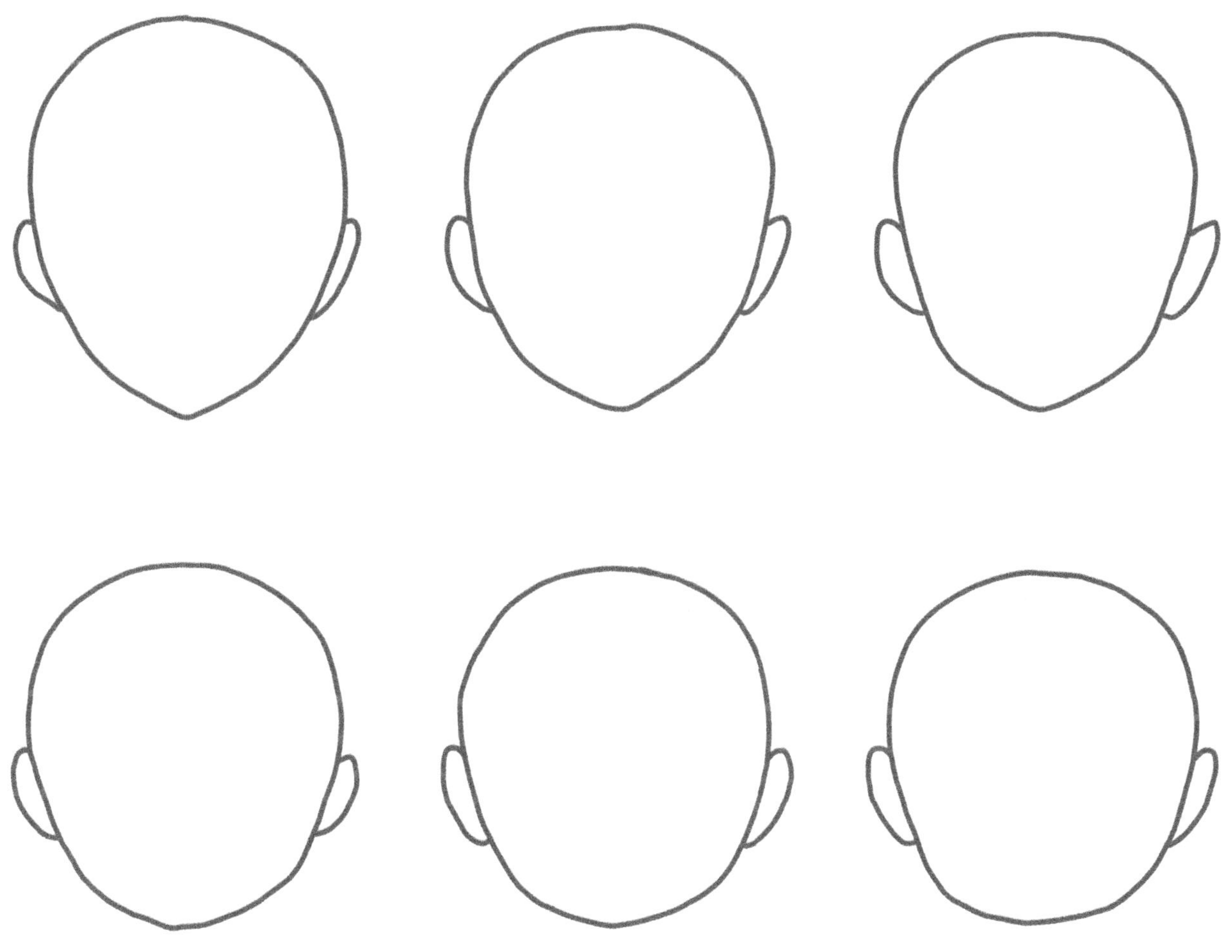

Heads should be drawn first before the eyes, hair, mouth or nose.

At first look these heads look basically the same, but with a closer look you can see differences between each of them. The small changes are what make characters look differenct from each other.

HEAD TYPES

The main changes in a head are the height between different types. There are two major types.

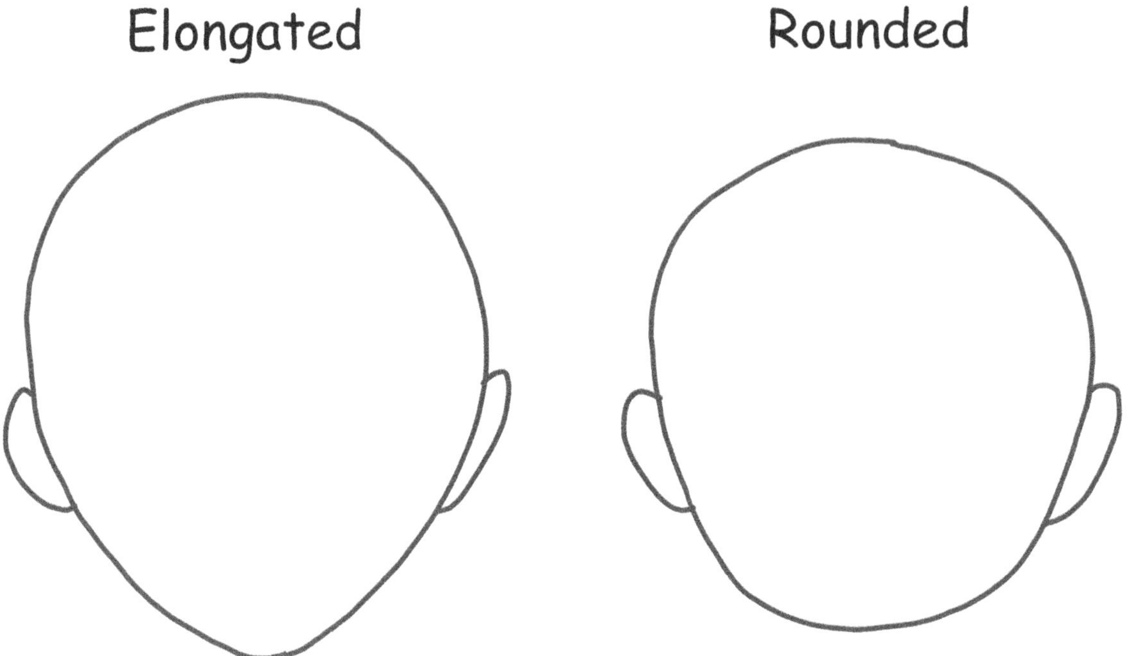

By making a head elongated it will give your character the appearance of being skinny and tall or both.

A rounded head makes a good style for short characters or children. You can also adjust the heights for women vs. men.

Pro-Tip: Changing the size of the ears can also increase the percieved height and width of the head.

Regardless of the head type you draw, always start with drawing a cross before anything else.

As you can see below, weather you are drawing a rounded or elongated head, a cross will help you find the center of the head.

The cross also marks important features on the face that will have to be drawn later.

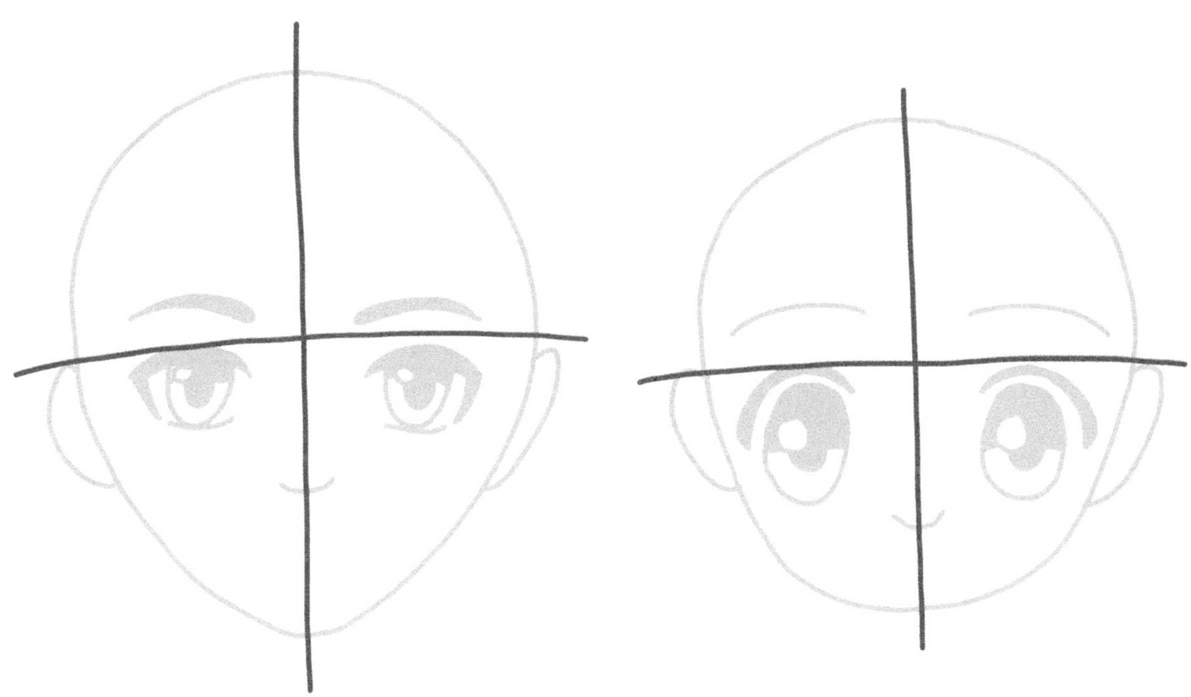

The cross marks the top of the ears, bottom of the eyebrows, and top of the eyeballs.

The vertical line will also mark the center of the nose and middle of the chin.

After you have drawn your cross, you'll then want to decide what type of head you will draw.

Once you know the size you want, draw lines where the top of the head is and the chin. Additionally draw lines where the side of the head will go.

Make sure the side lines are the head, and not where the ears will go.

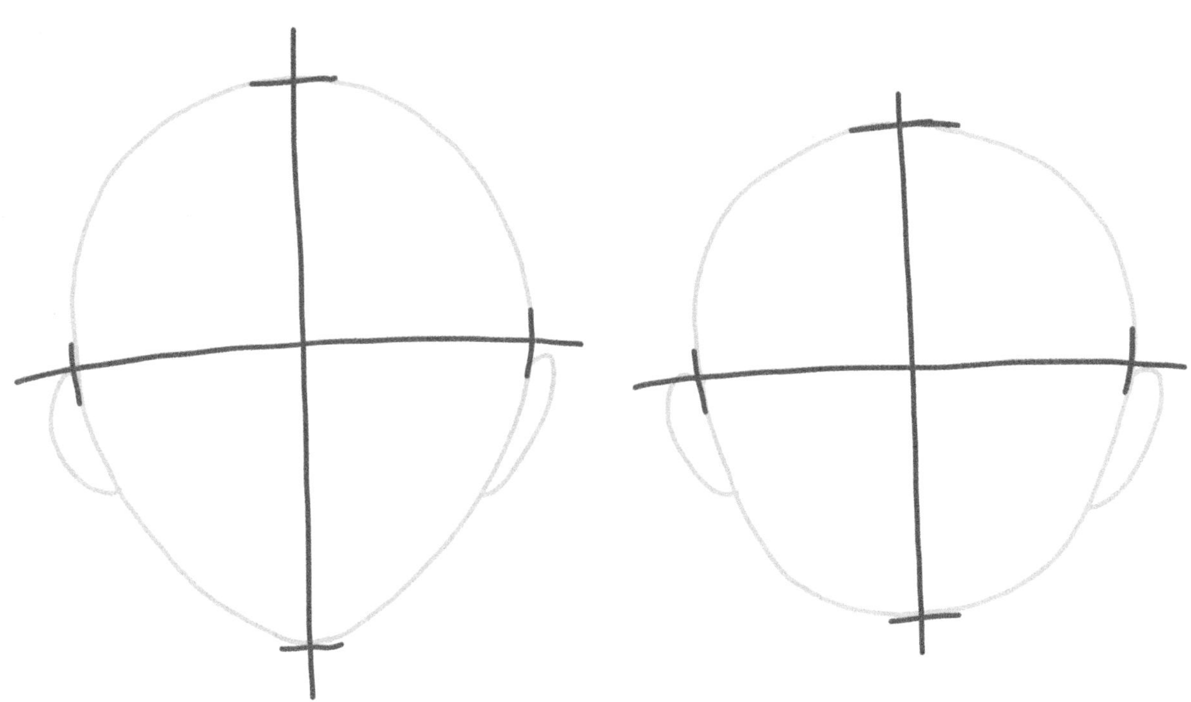

By drawing the lines first you can have a guide to connect the entire circle or oval of the head together.

Last of all connect the lines together to form your head.

Practice Makes Perfect! Use the page below to practice drawing what you have learned so far.

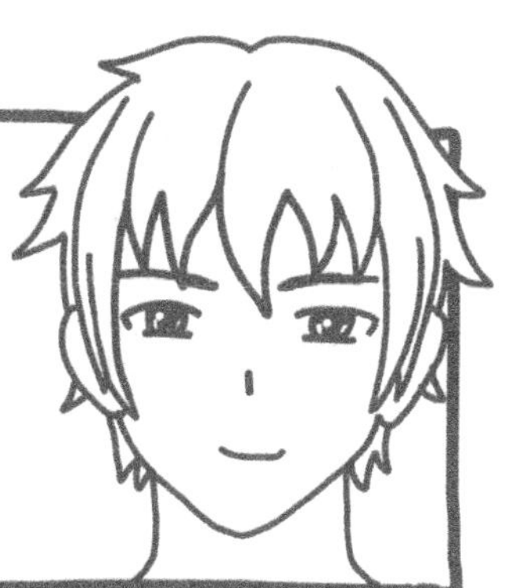

CHIN TYPES

For now your heads probably look like circles or ovals. This is normal since we haven't made any changes to the chins.

The chins will change the head type to be a more rounded or pointed head. you can have a rounded head with a pointed chin or rounded chin. The same goes for an elongated head.

Pointed Chin   Rounded Chin

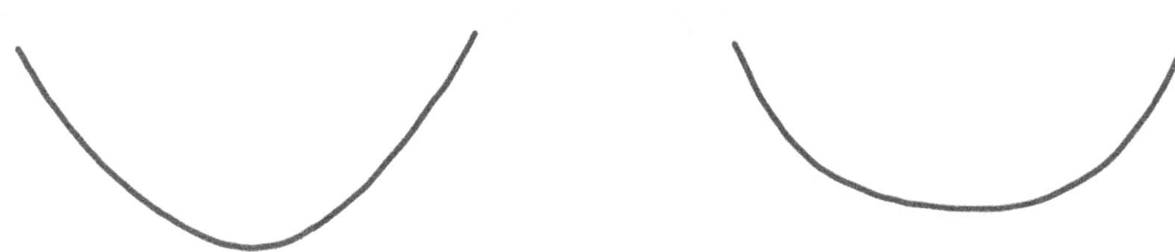

Changing the face type is as easy as changing the chin. You can experiment by using different chins on different head styles.

Try a pointed chin on a rounded head to get a different look than a rounded chin on a rounded head.

Practice drawing chins on each of the heads below. Start by drawing a line where you want the chin.

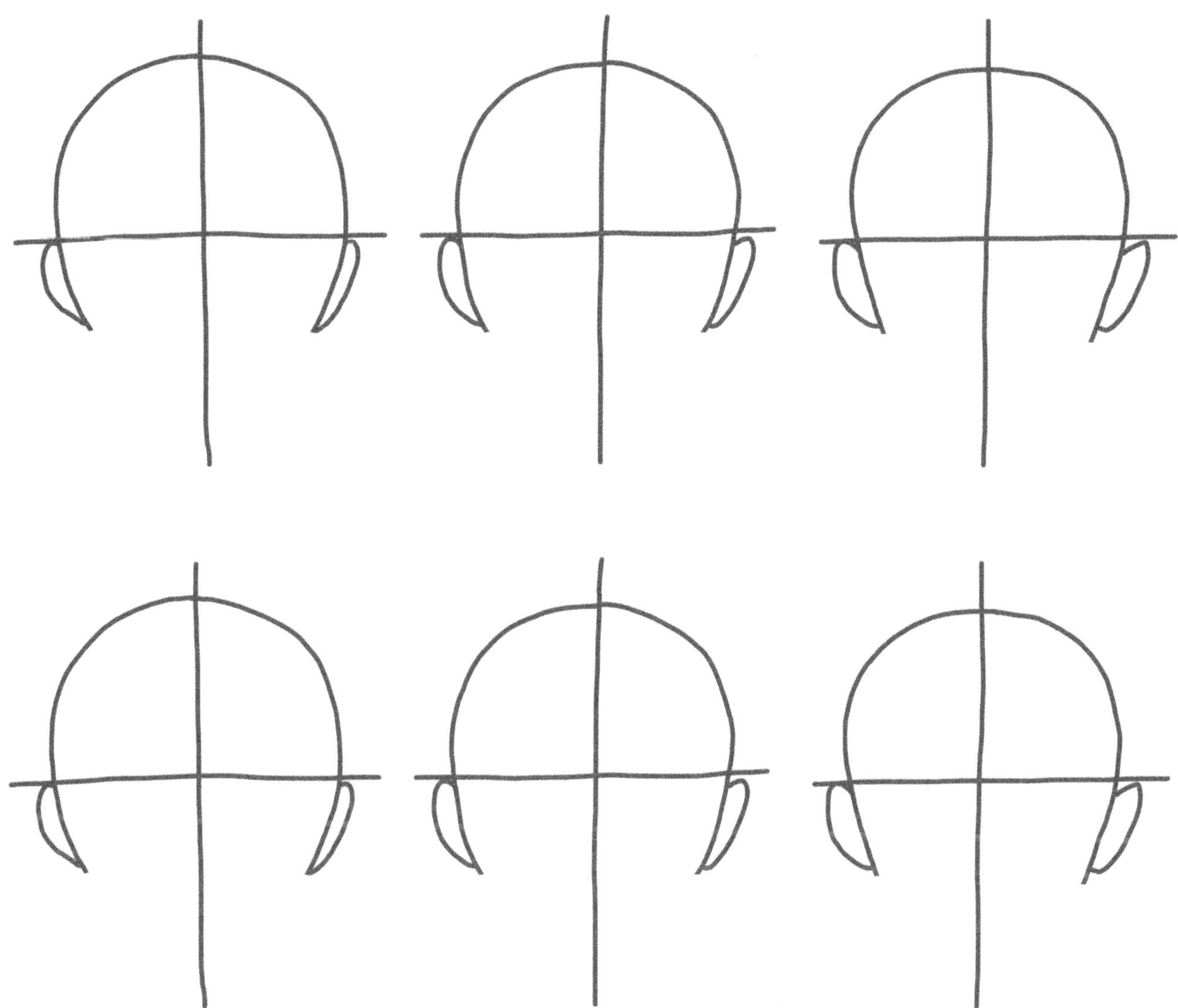

Next connect the sides of the face to the chin line you have drawn.

Do different chin types from rounded to elongated and everything inbetween. Each head should look a little different.

Practice Makes Perfect! Use the page below to practice drawing what you have learned so far.

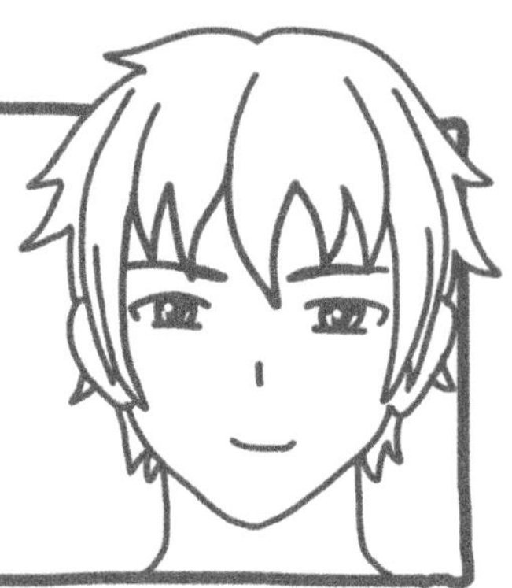

EARS

The last part of the head that can change is the ears. Ears generally have two variations as well with many options between those variations.

Bigger on the Bottom Bigger on the Top

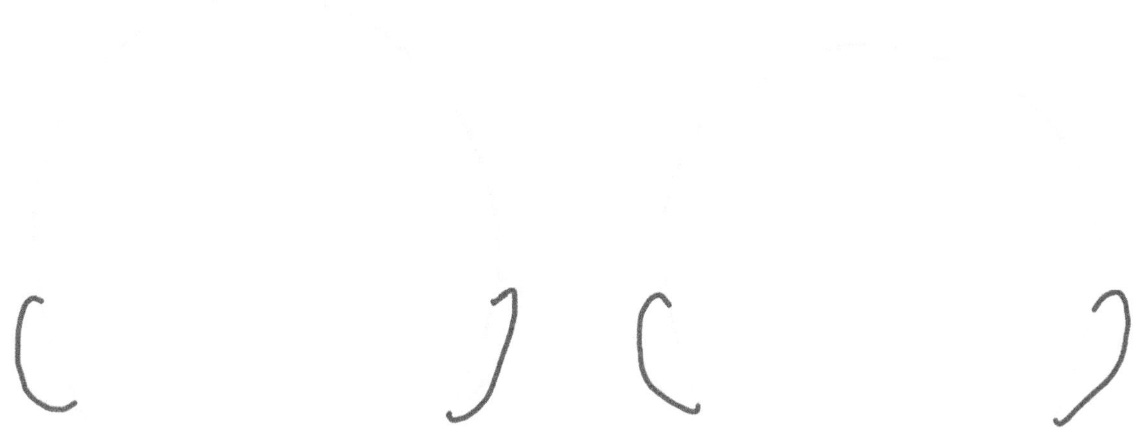

Ears have usually a more rounded part on the top or bottom of the ear.

On the left head you'll see a rounded bottom and on the right you'll see a rounded top.

Some ears can also be rounded in the middle. You can change the location of the rounded part based on your liking. There is no specific ear for a specific head type. Some anime drawings have no rounded part.

Practice drawing ears on the different head types below. If it helps you can draw a cross on the heads first to determine where the ears should go on the heads.

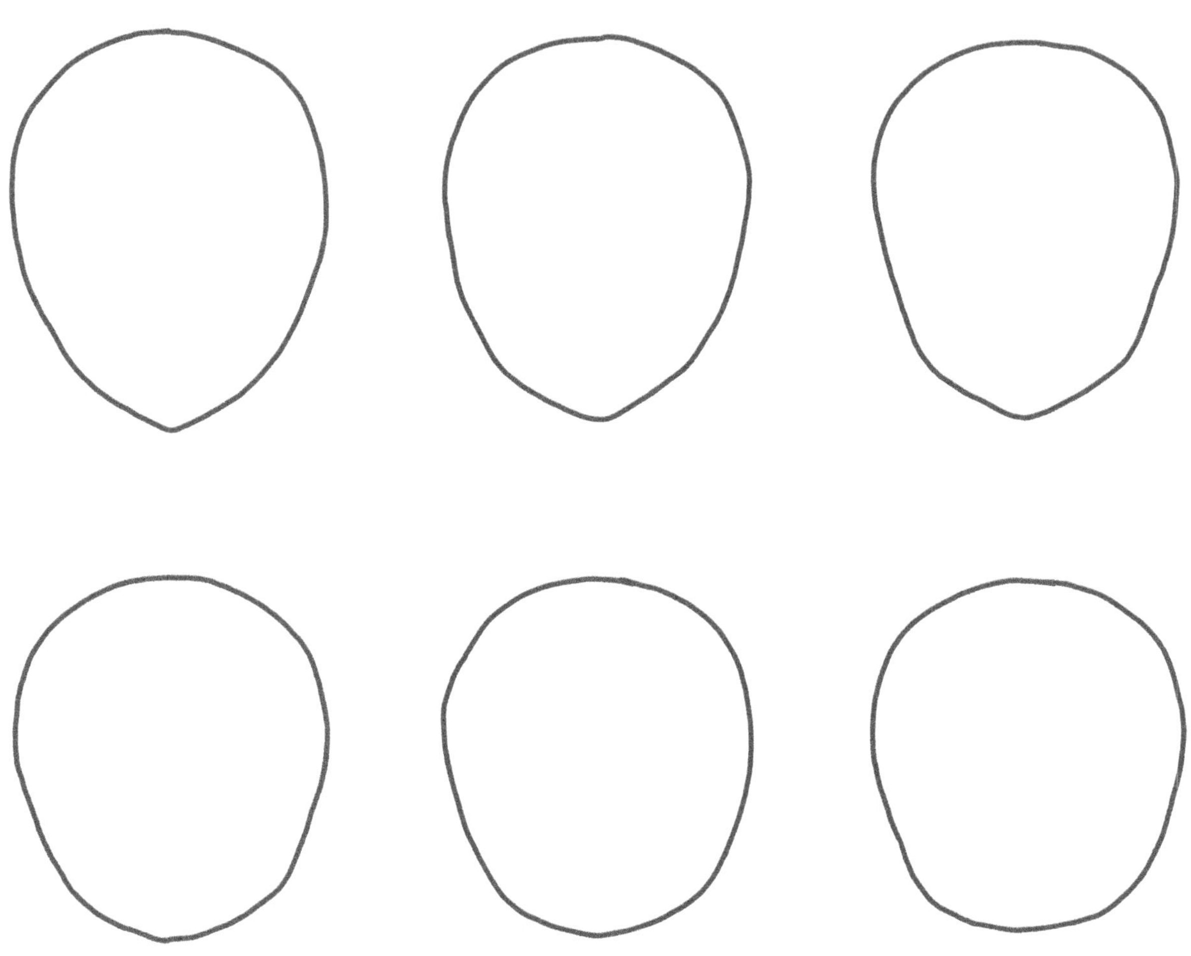

The top of the ears should go just below the bottom of the cross part of the "t".

You can move the ears anywhere you want but the correct position to line up properly with eyes etc. is below the cross.

Practice Makes Perfect! Use the page below to practice drawing what you have learned so far.

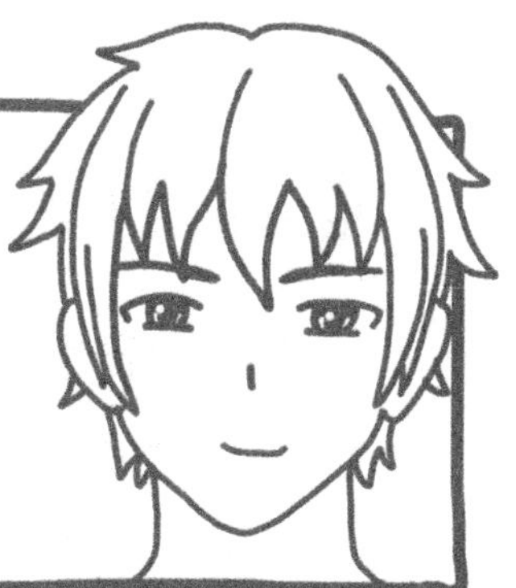

CONCLUSION

The head is the main canvas that you will be working on throughout this book on drawing anime. A properly drawn head will make adding details like eyes, ears, nose, mouth and hair much easier.

Go back and continue to practice drawing different head shapes to get better at it.

Make sure to draw all head types while using different ears and chins on your characters.

As you continue to practice you'll find it becoming easier and easier to get the results you desire.

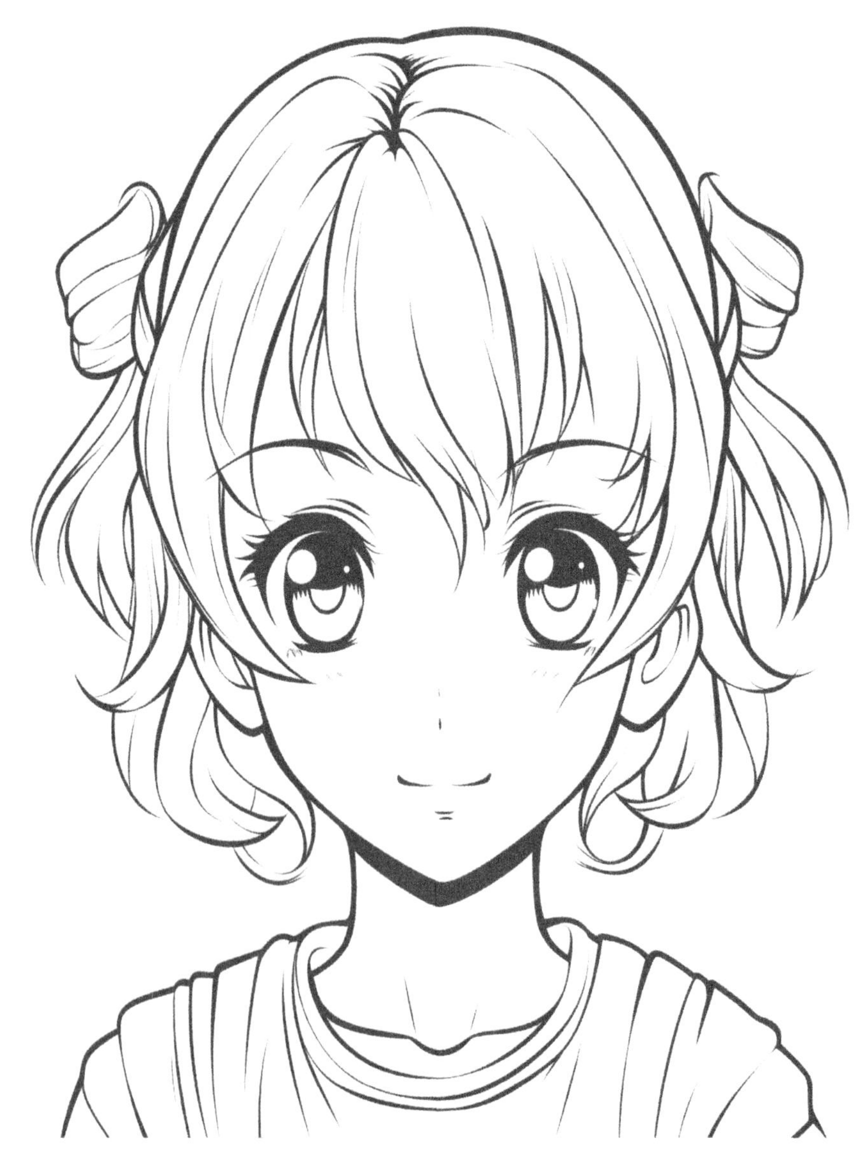

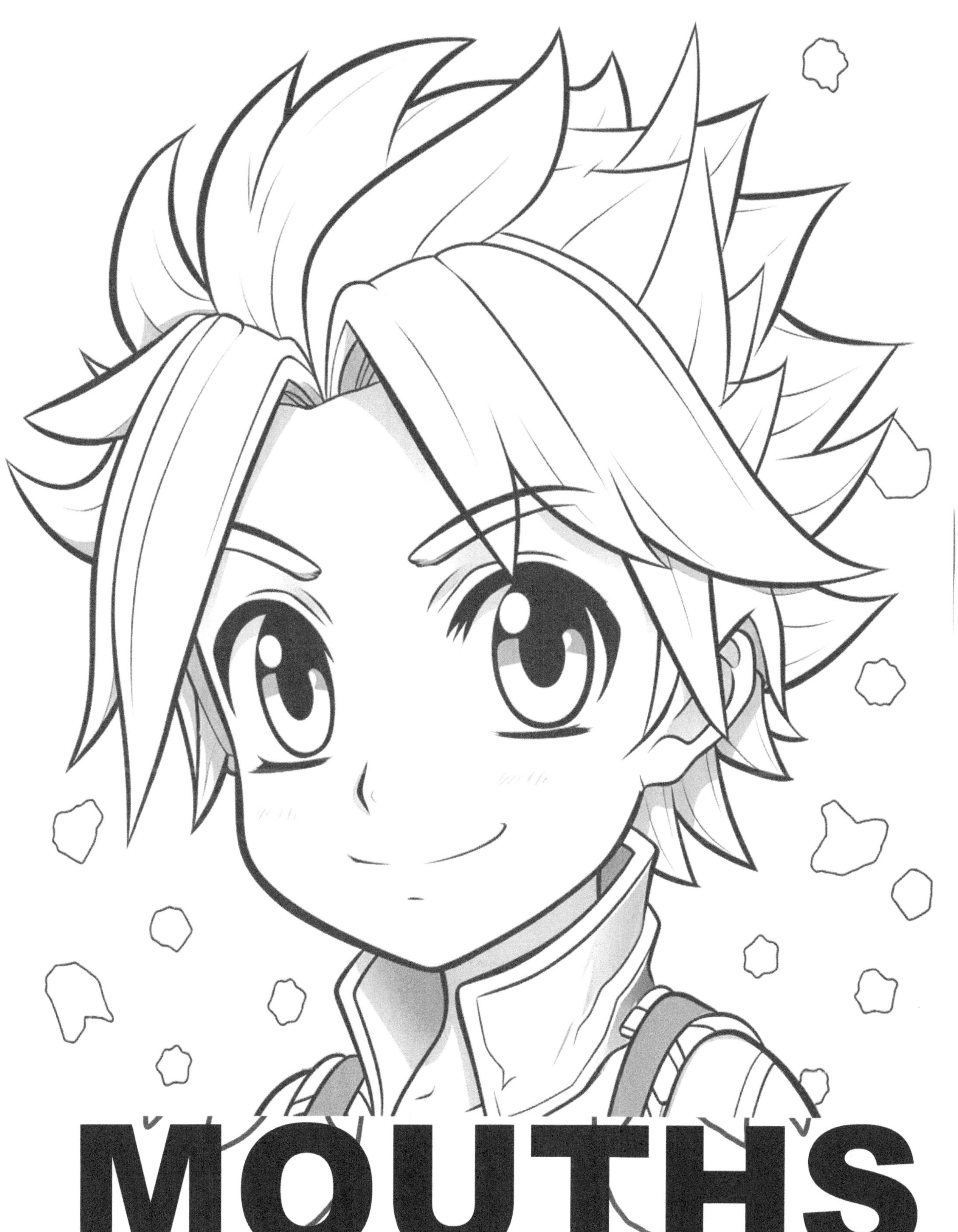

MOUTHS

MOUTHS

There are too many types of mouths to list them all. Here are just a few.

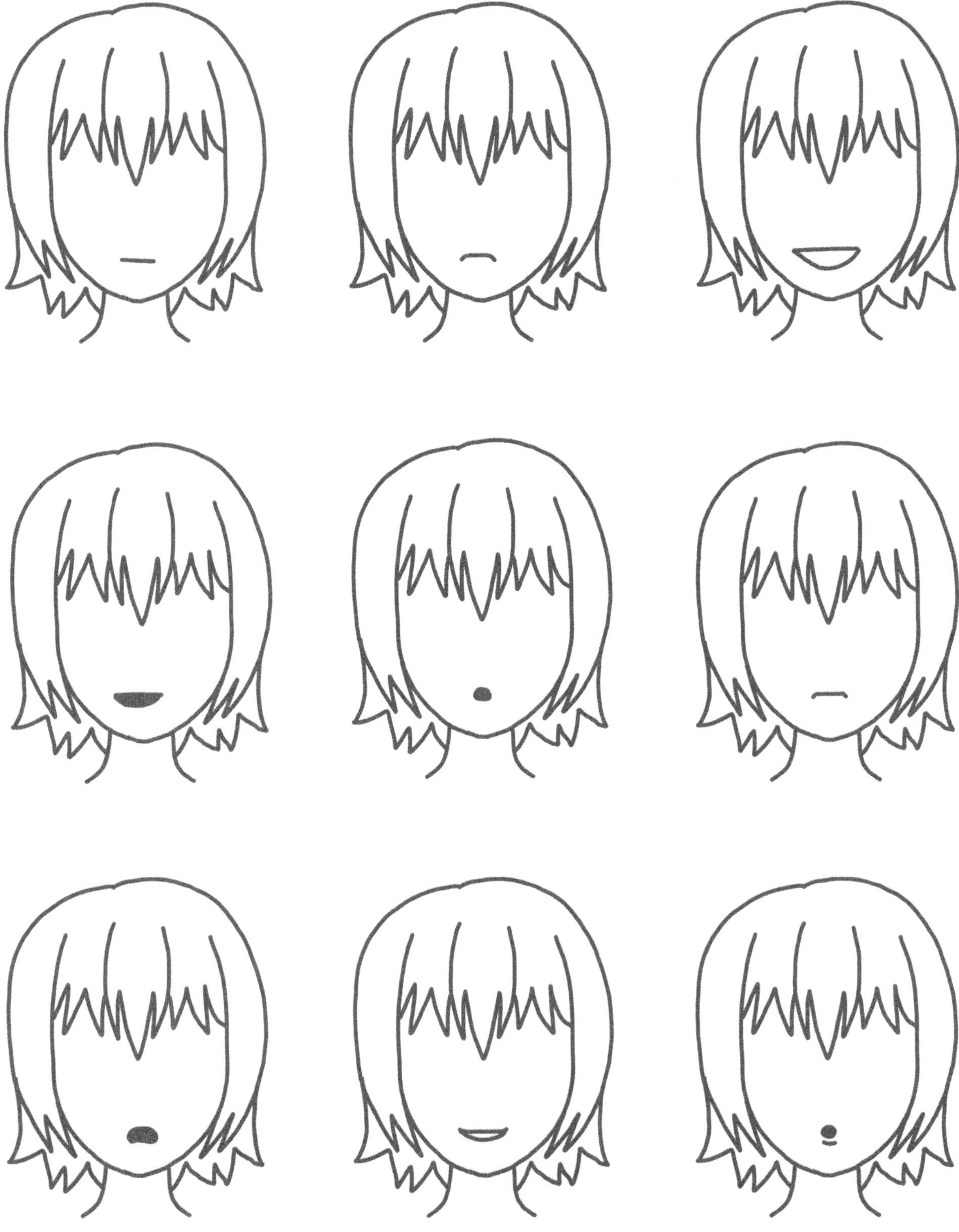

Mouths in anime are meant to be more of a secondary feature vs. something like the eyes which are primary.

Watch how we can change the complete expression of a character just by changing the eyes, but do nothing with the mouth.

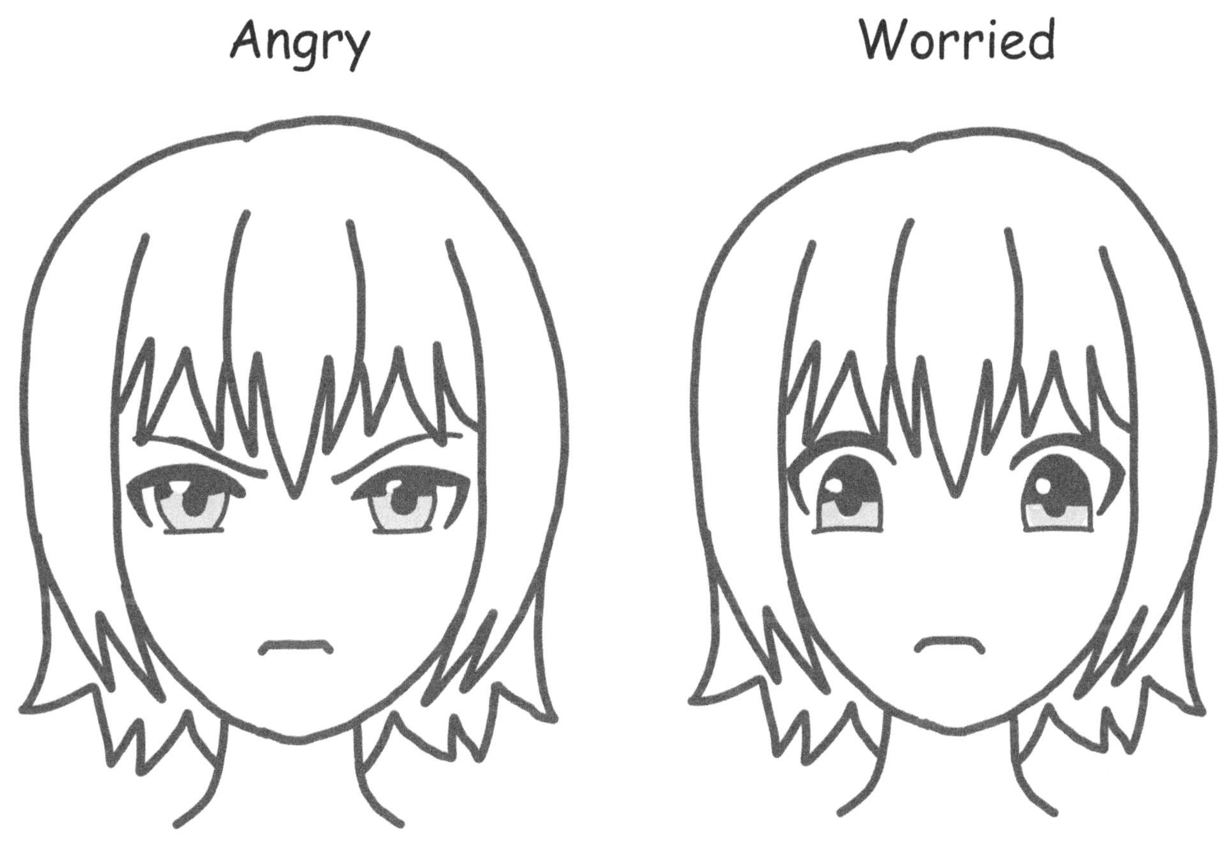

At first glance before reading you may not have noticed the mouths didn't change at all. At a closer look though you'll see that the mouths are identical along with the hair and face but the eyes make the character completely change emotions and therfore the whole face looks different.

Since we know that the mouth shape is meant to support the expression of the eyes, we need to determine the shape based on how your character is feeling.

Before we do that however we have to find the right place to put the mouth on your character. You can do that with a couple of steps.

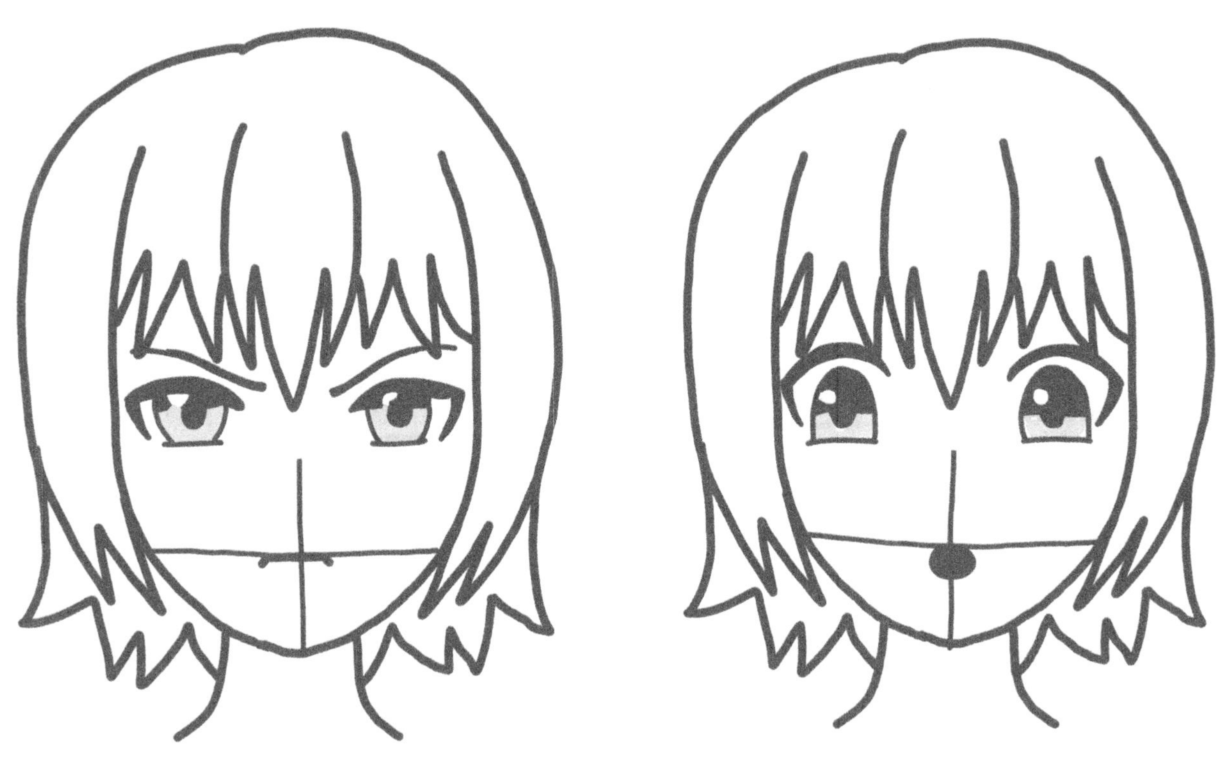

From the drawings above you'll see that the mouth should be just below the center of a cross. It should also be centered on the vertical line. Draw the cross mid-way between the bottom of the eyes and the chin. The vertical line should be centered in the middle of the head.

Practice drawing mouths below. Don't worry about the shape but instead the correct placement.

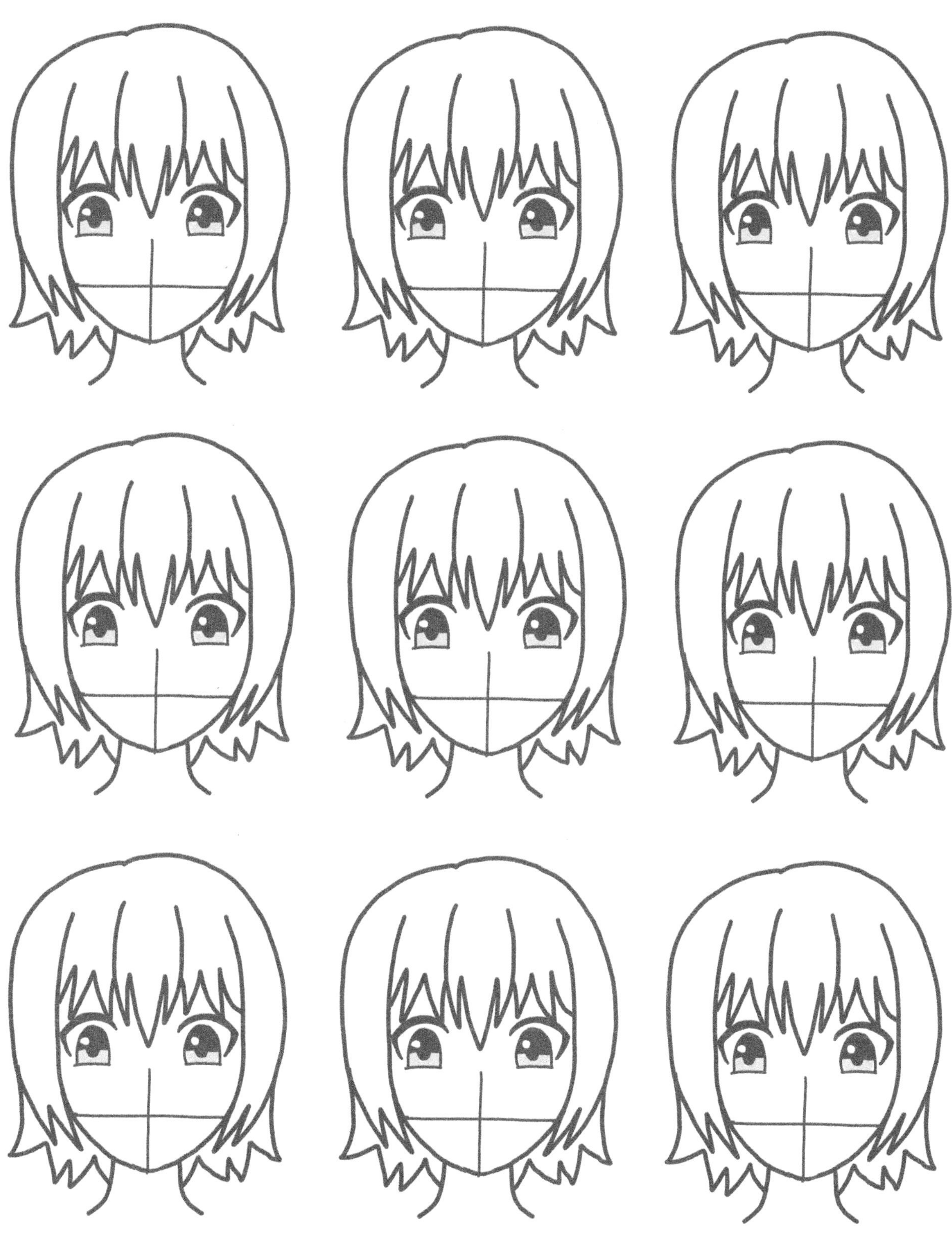

Practice Makes Perfect! Use the page below to practice drawing what you have learned so far.

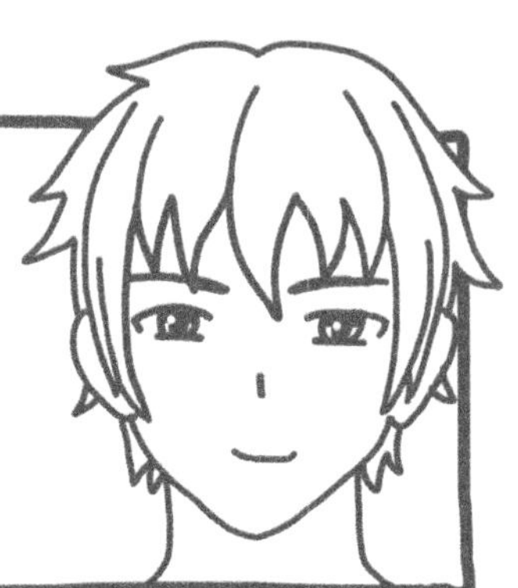

Now let's talk about mouth types. There are three main mouth types in anime:

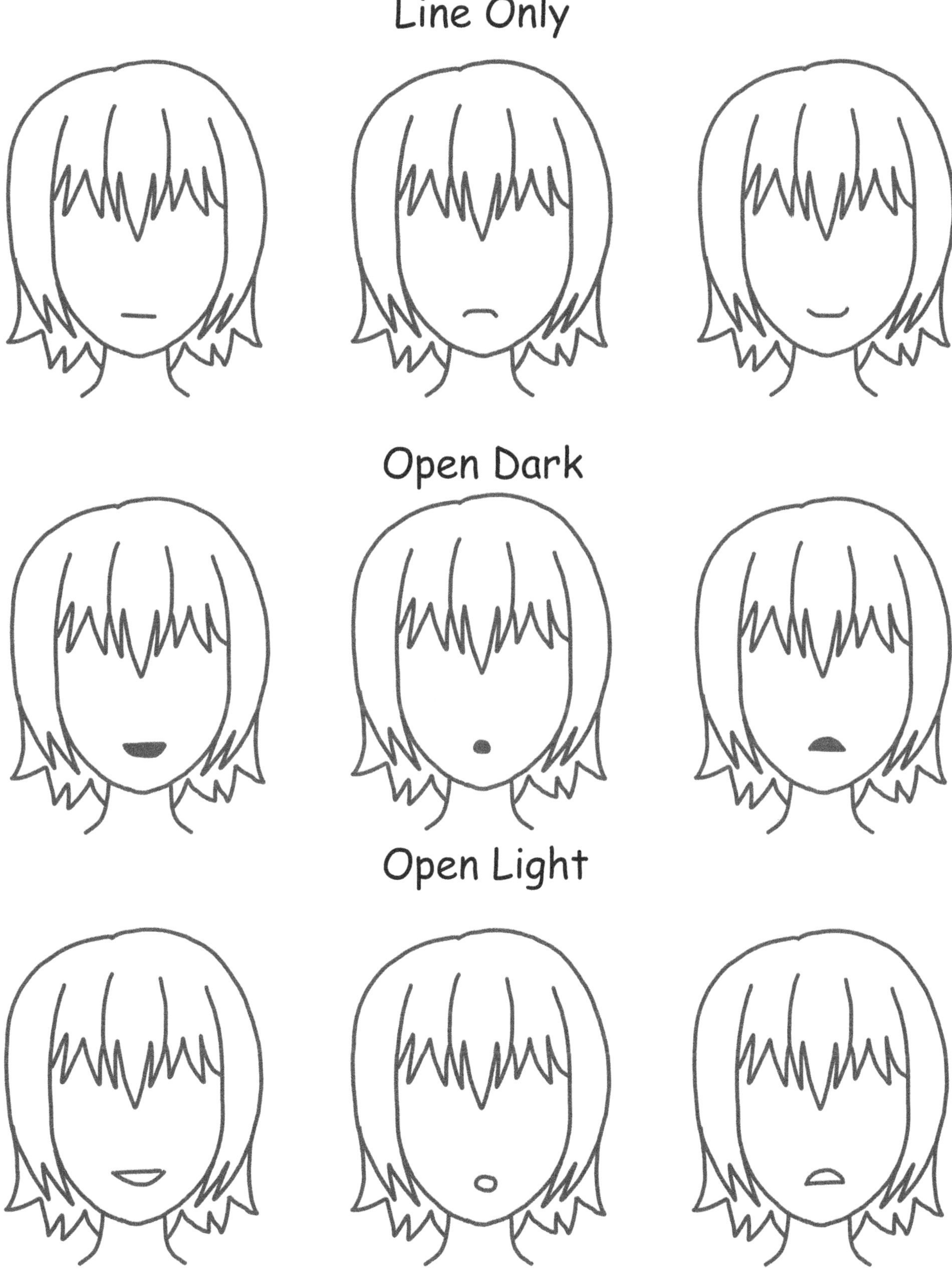

LINE-ONLY

Line-only mouths are the most basic to draw. No matter the shape the mouth is one line.

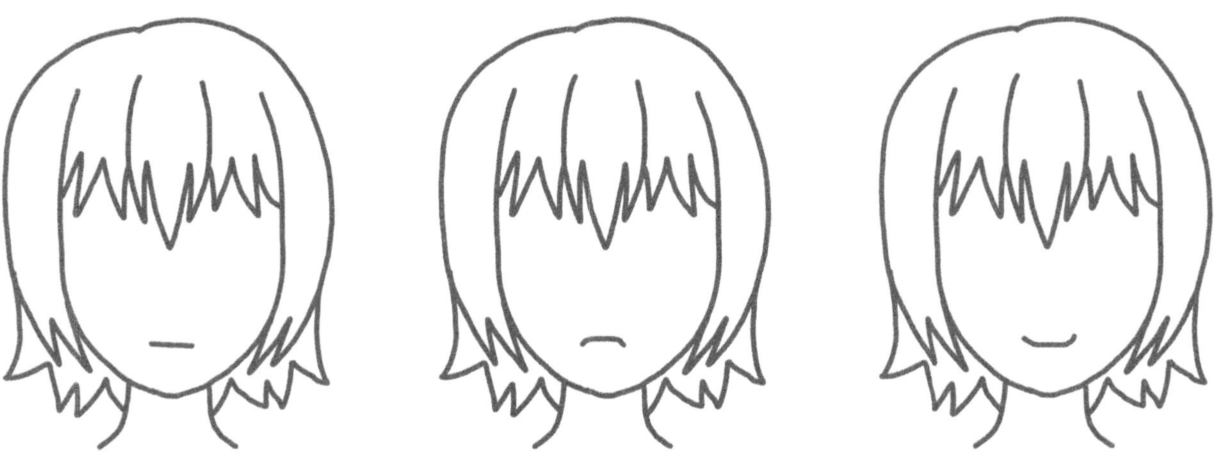

Practice drawing line-only mouths below. Use a variation of sad, happy, mad etc.

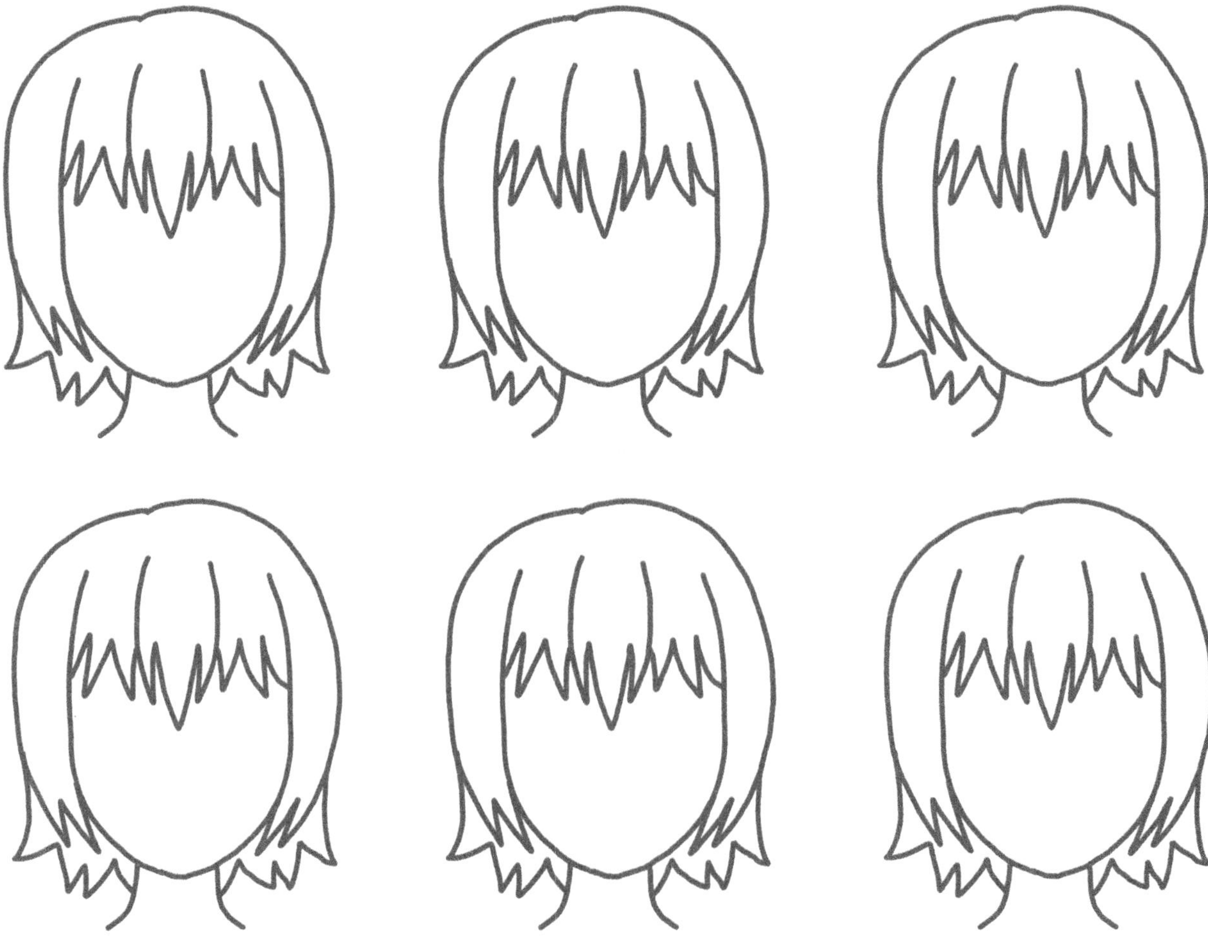

Practice makes perfect. Draw Line-Only mouths in the faces below:

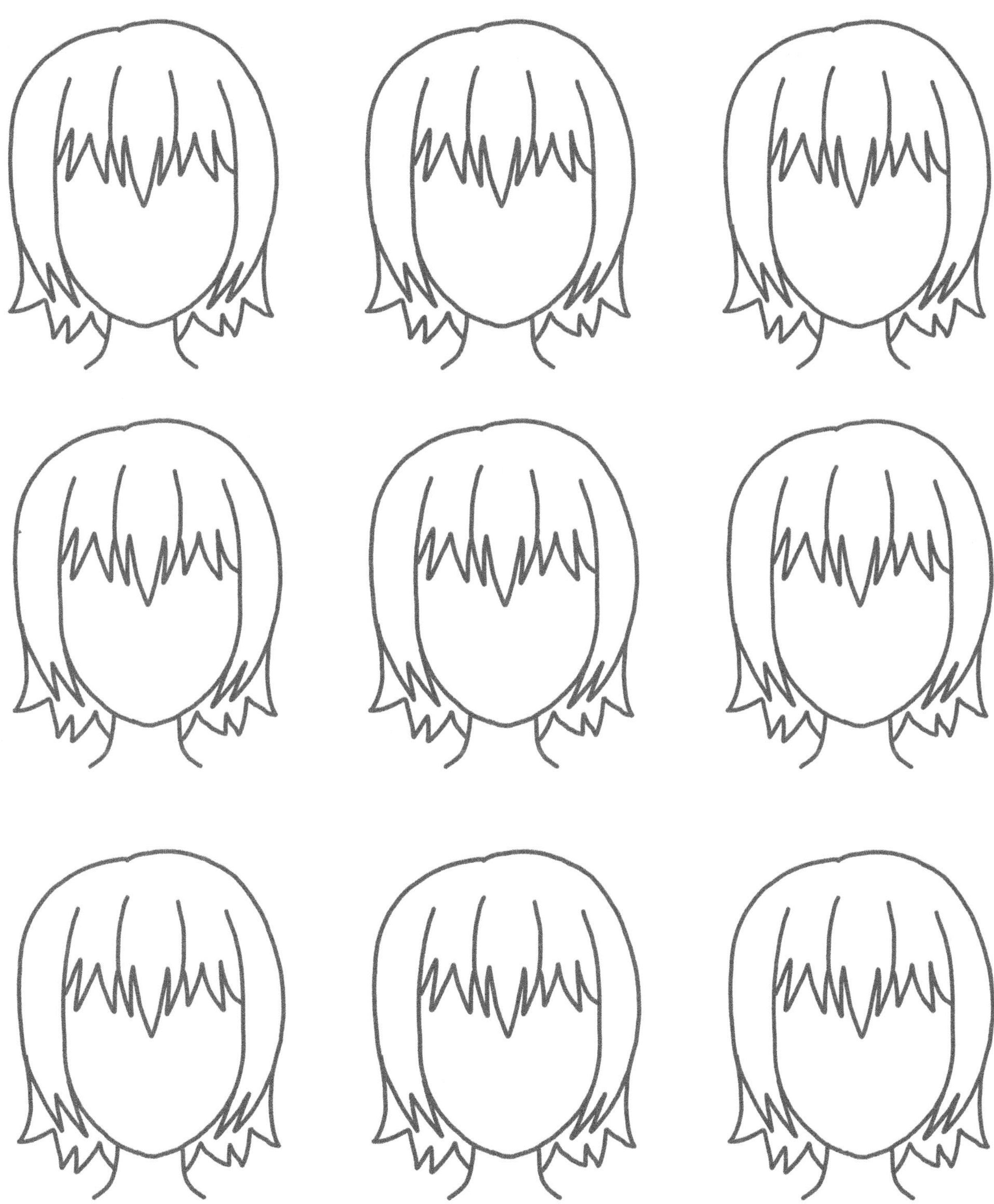

Practice Makes Perfect! Use the page below to practice drawing what you have learned so far.

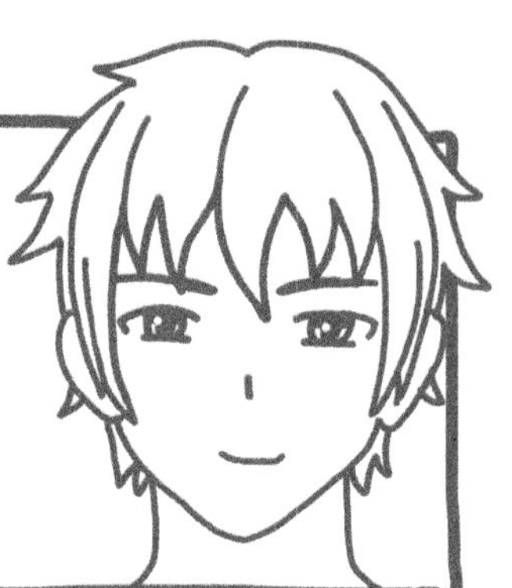

OPEN-LIGHT

This type of mouth requires two lines. Use open light for laughing, talking, joy etc. To draw the open mouth start with the one-line approach but for either the top or bottom lip, then add a second line for the opposite lip.

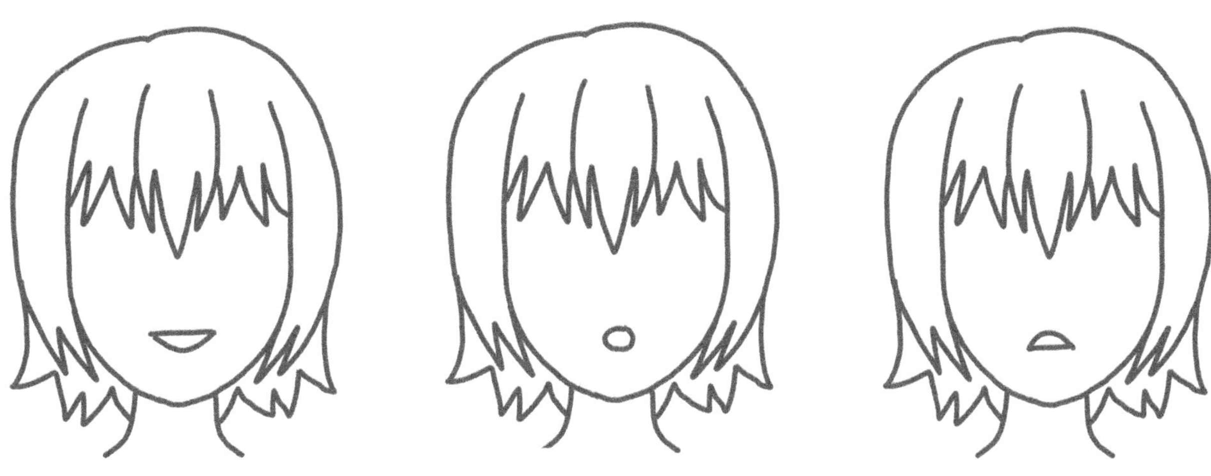

Open light is the most difficult to draw because you have to account for the top and bottom lips.

You also can't easily hide mistakes with this type of mouth so your lines need to be as precise as possible. The mouth is somewhat easy to draw when you get the handle on it, remember to keep it simple since the mouth isn't one of the main features.

Pro-Tip: When drawing any mouth, look in the mirror and change your expression, then use that expression in your drawing.

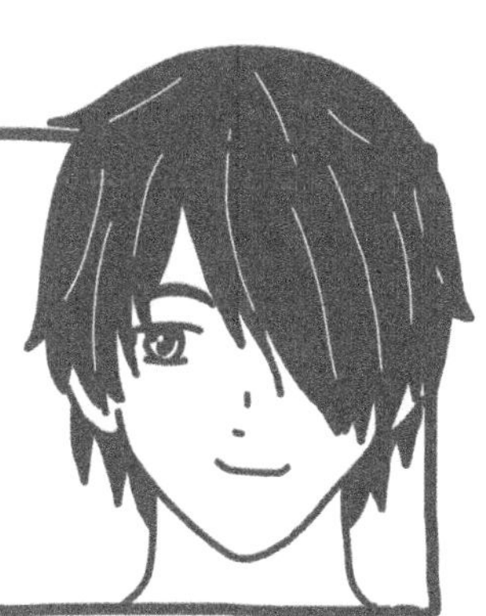

Practice makes perfect. Draw Open-Light mouths in the faces below:

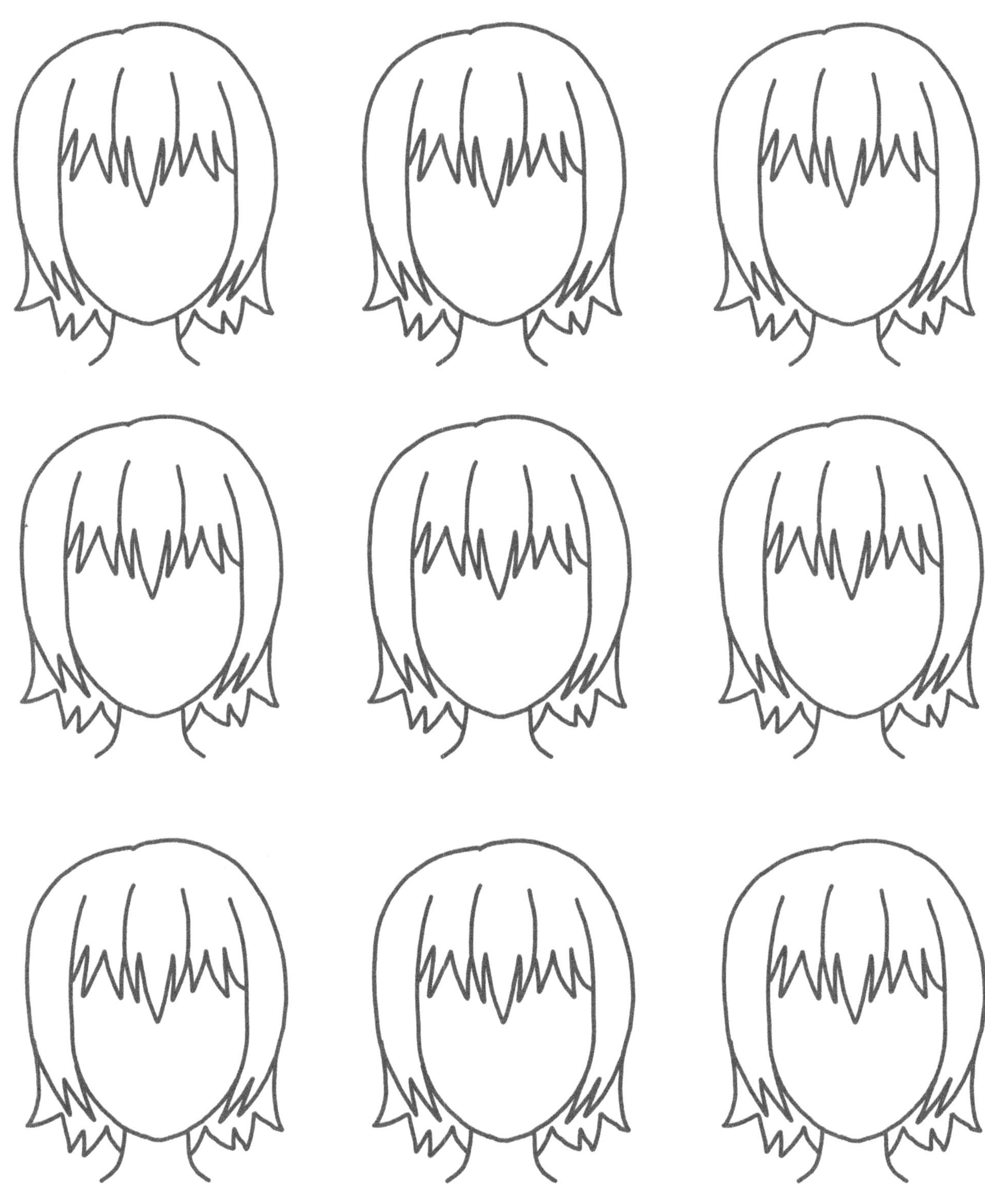

Practice Makes Perfect! Use the page below to practice drawing what you have learned so far.

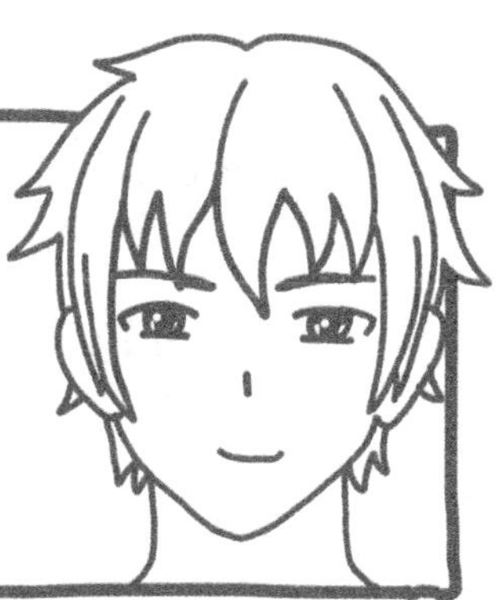

OPEN-DARK

This style is the same as open-light but with the mouth filled in with pen. Use this for talking, laughing, surprise, etc.

When you draw open-dark, start with and open light mouth and then fill in the area. Usually open dark is used for emotions like sadness, anger, bad surprises and more.

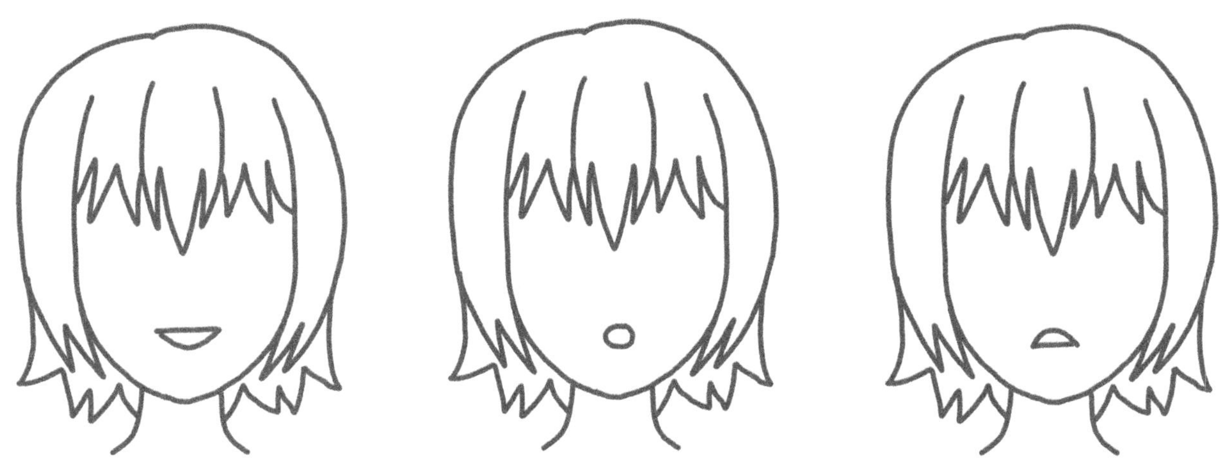

As you compare the same mouth shapes for open-light and open dark, imagine the differences in emotion that would work for each style.

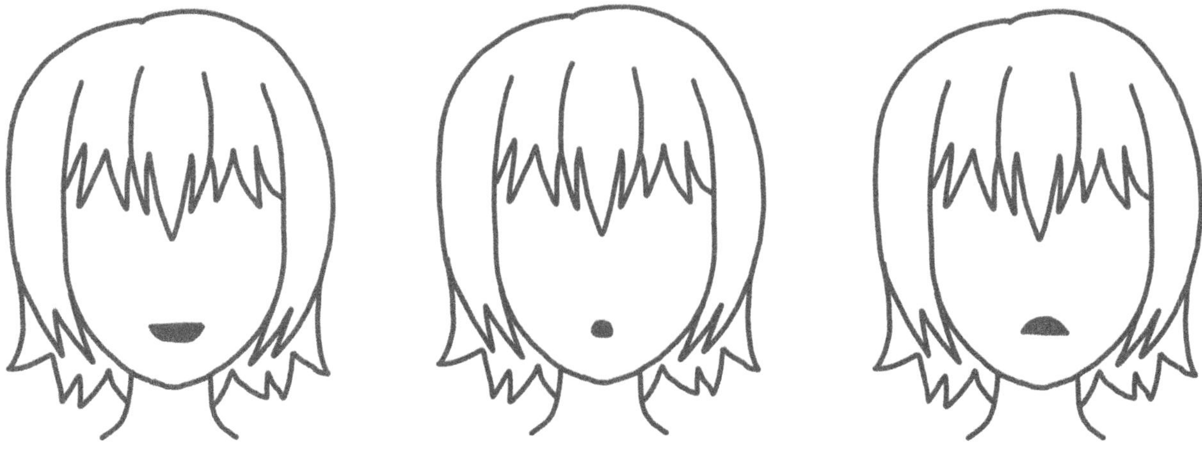

Practice makes perfect. Draw Open-Dark mouths in the faces below:

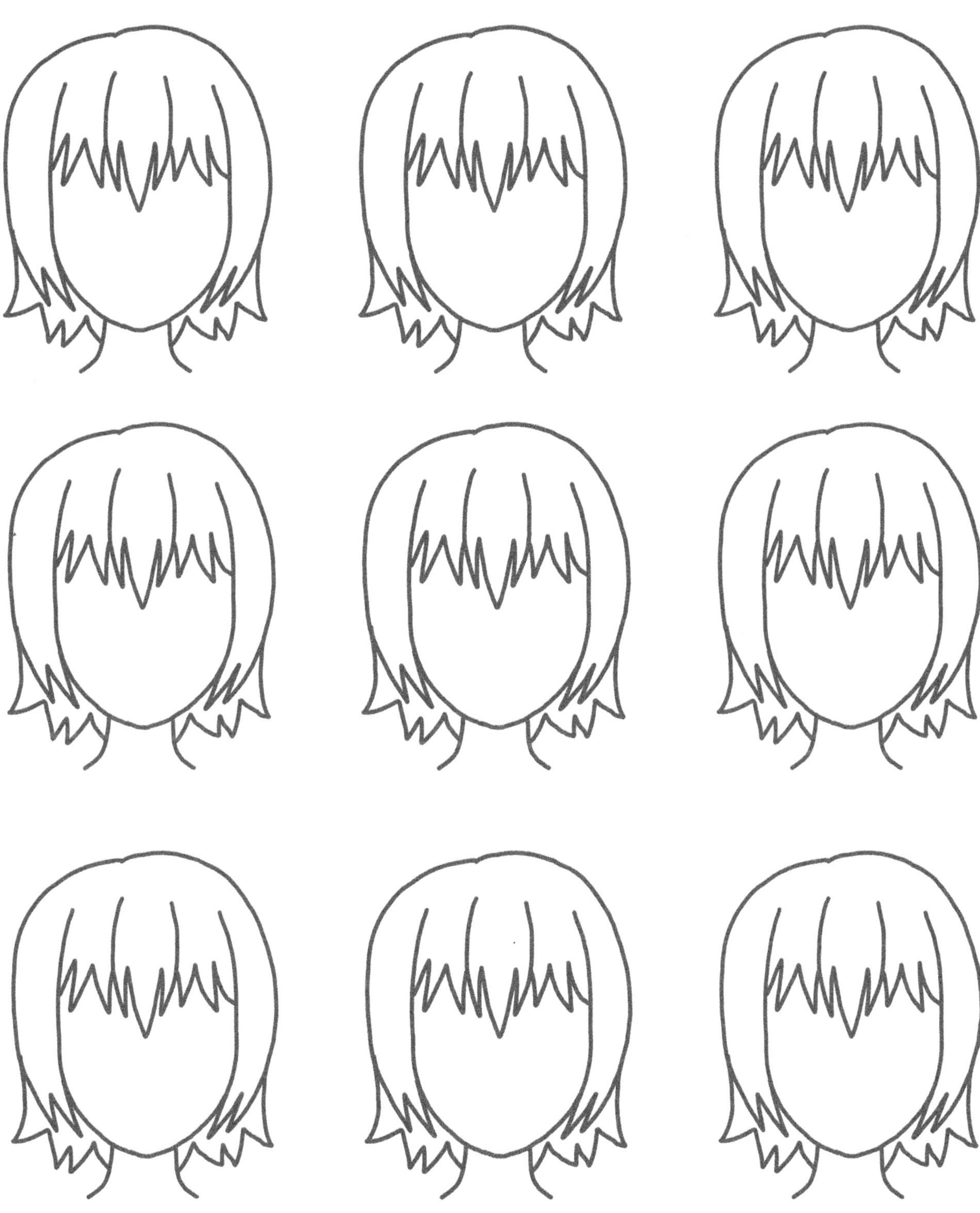

Practice Makes Perfect! Use the page below to practice drawing what you have learned so far.

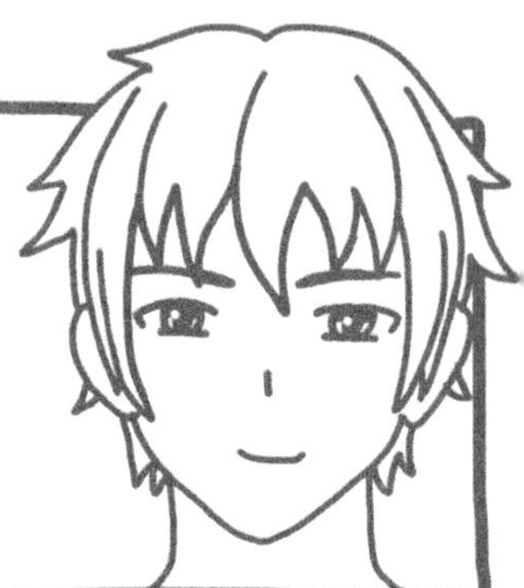

CONCLUSION

The mouth is a part of the head that adds just a little expression to the entire face. Use the mouth to show the emotion of the face but mainly to support the emotion already being shown by the eyes.

As you practice drawing mouths focus on making them fit in the correct areas so that your anime character will look realistic and well done.

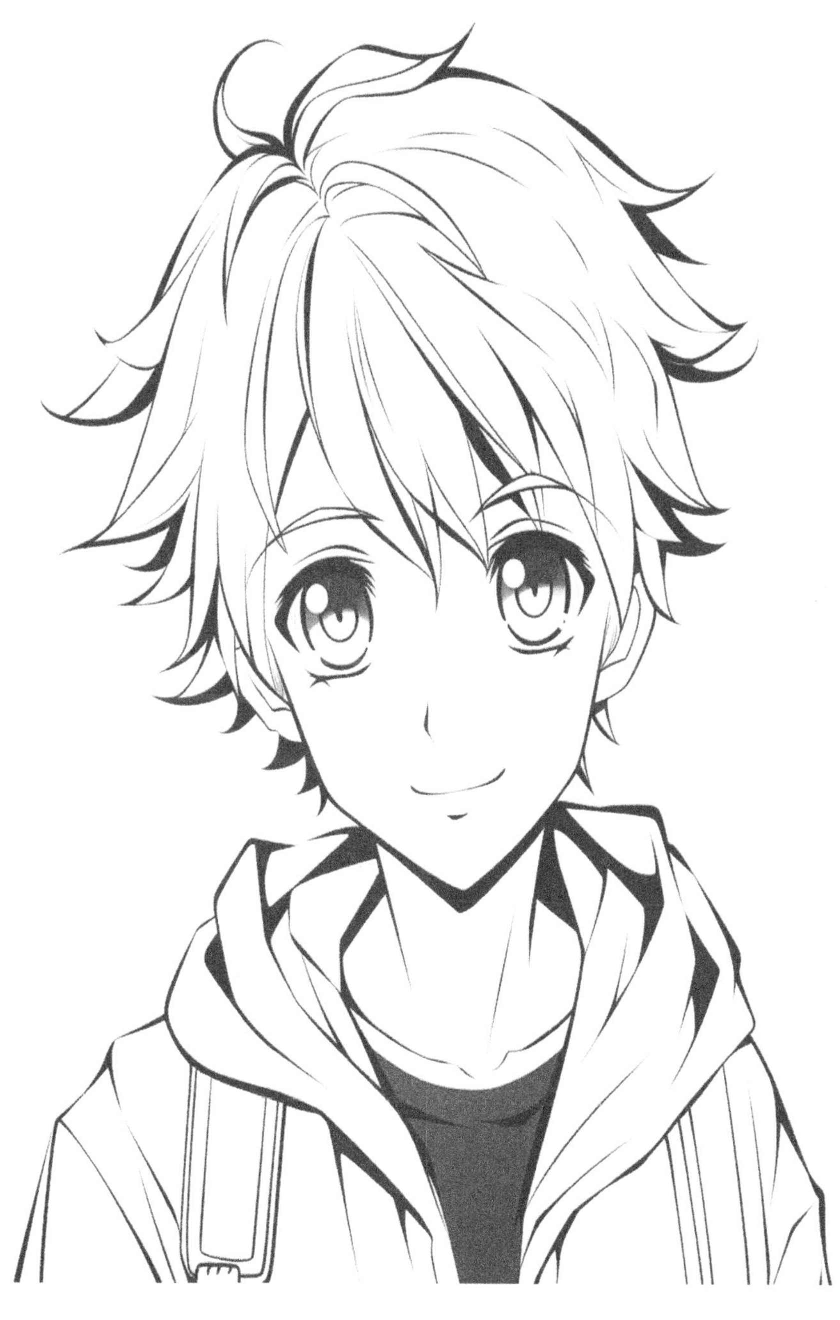

Like all anime drawing, the mouth takes a lot of practice while learning to draw. Keep practicing and your skills will continue to grow.

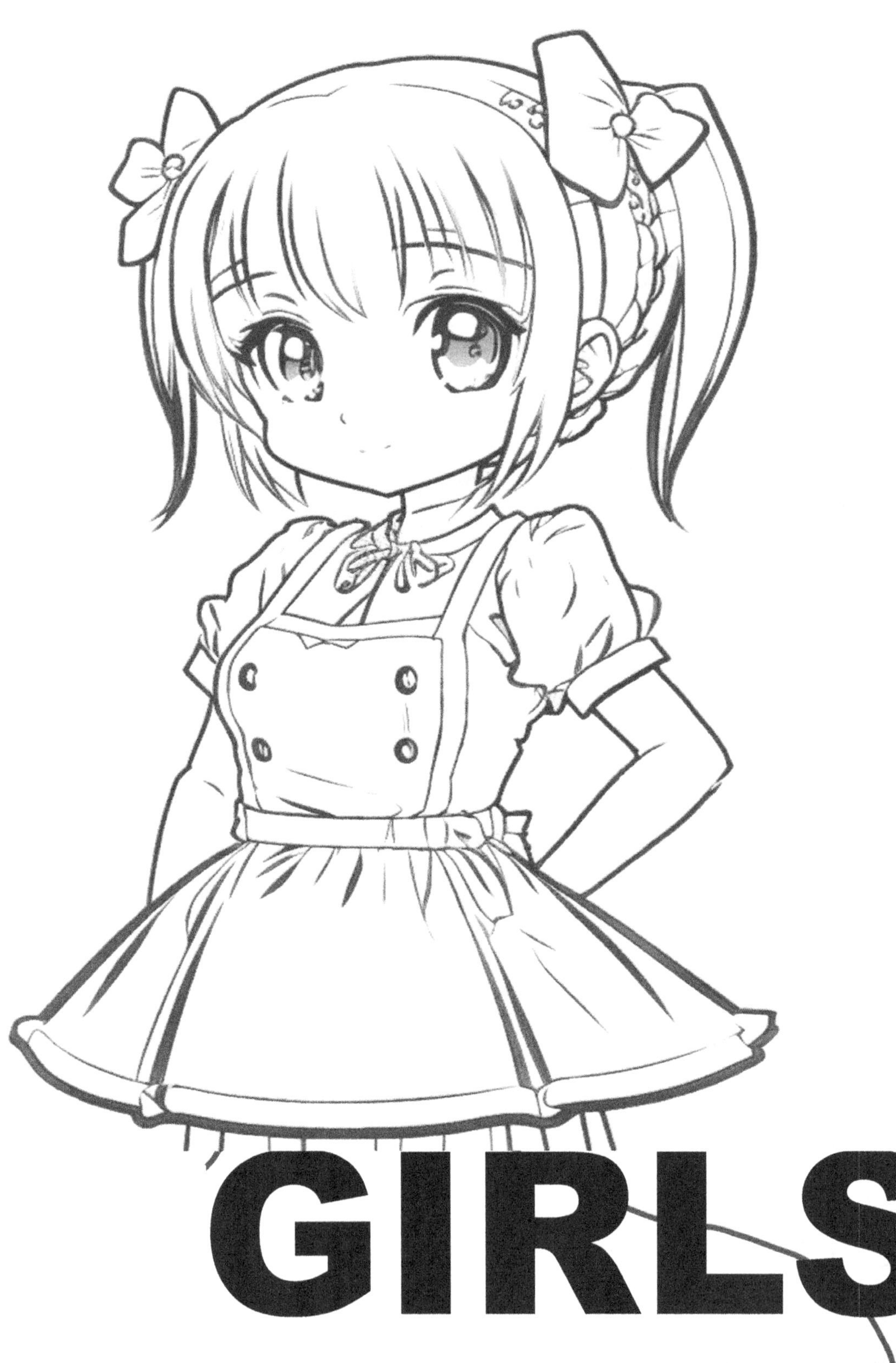

GIRLS HAIR

GIRLS HAIR

There are many different hair styles for anime girls. Teaching them all wouldn't be possible.

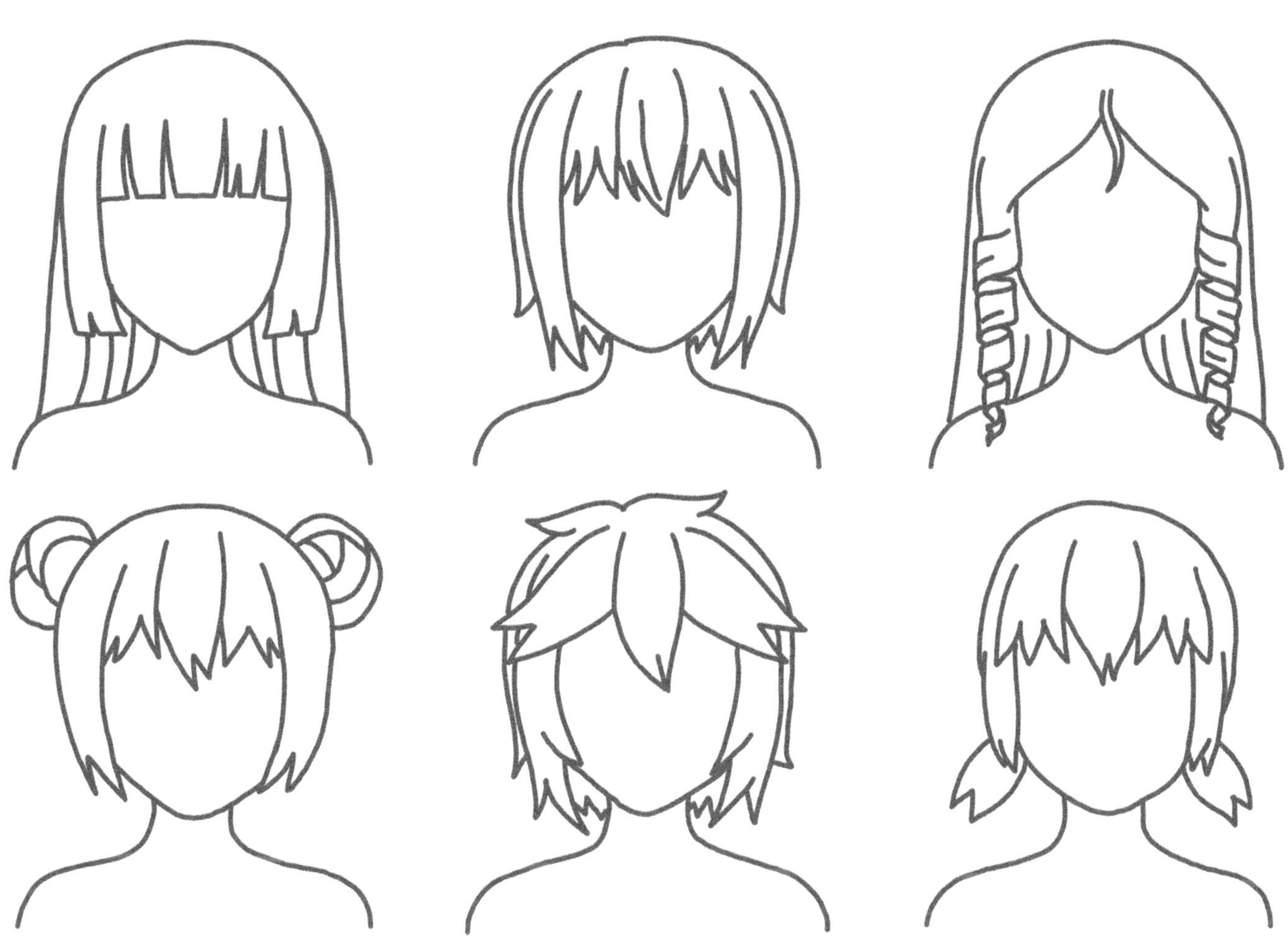

Hair is arguably the hardest part of the head to draw in an anime character. This is due to the detail required and importance of symmetry with the head shape and other features.

We'll cover the basics of drawing hair on anime girl characters in this section. The goal is not to show specific hair styles, but instead principles that will allow you to draw many styles.

Hair generally follows the contour of the face. Start with drawing a line that will be the edge of the hair around the head with a small space. This should be the outside of the hair.

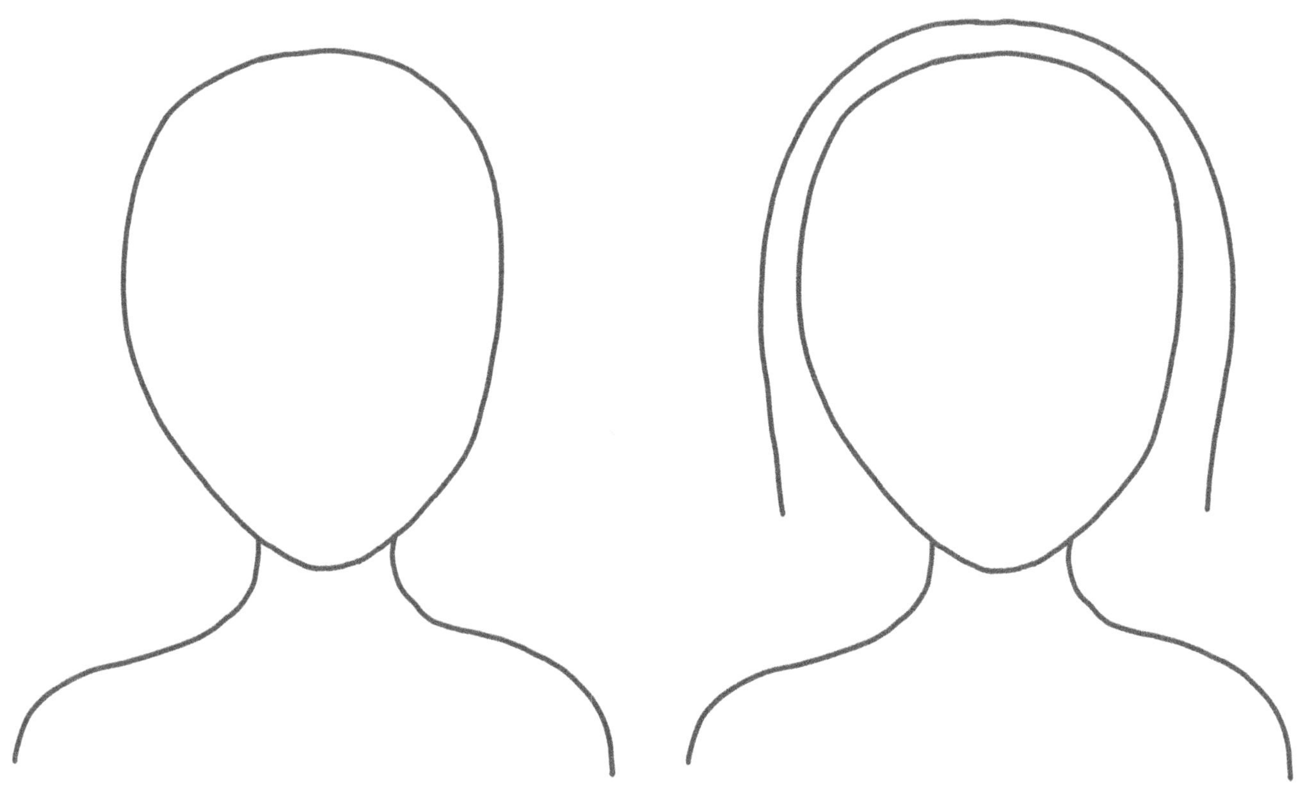

Then anywhere you want the hair to have more volume add in a little more space like at the bottom of the hair where the hair will reach to touch the shoulders.

Pro-Tip: Hair is about flow and detail. Practice your strokes over and over to get better at drawing smooth hair.

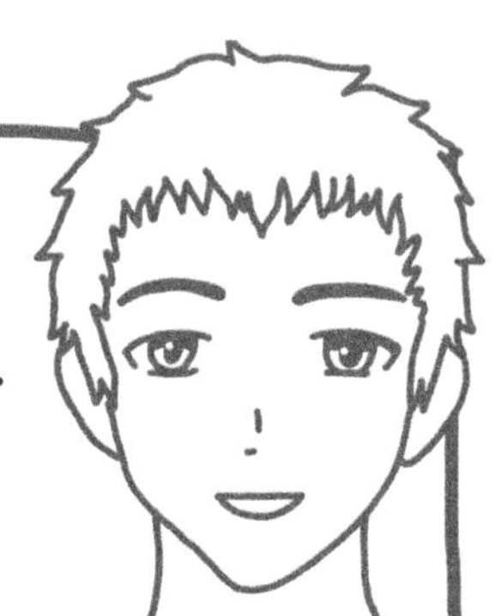

Once you have the outline of your hair, you can add detail. In most cases you can draw the detail of the hair on just half of the head. Once it looks how you like you can just copy or fold the paper in half and trace it on the other side of the head.

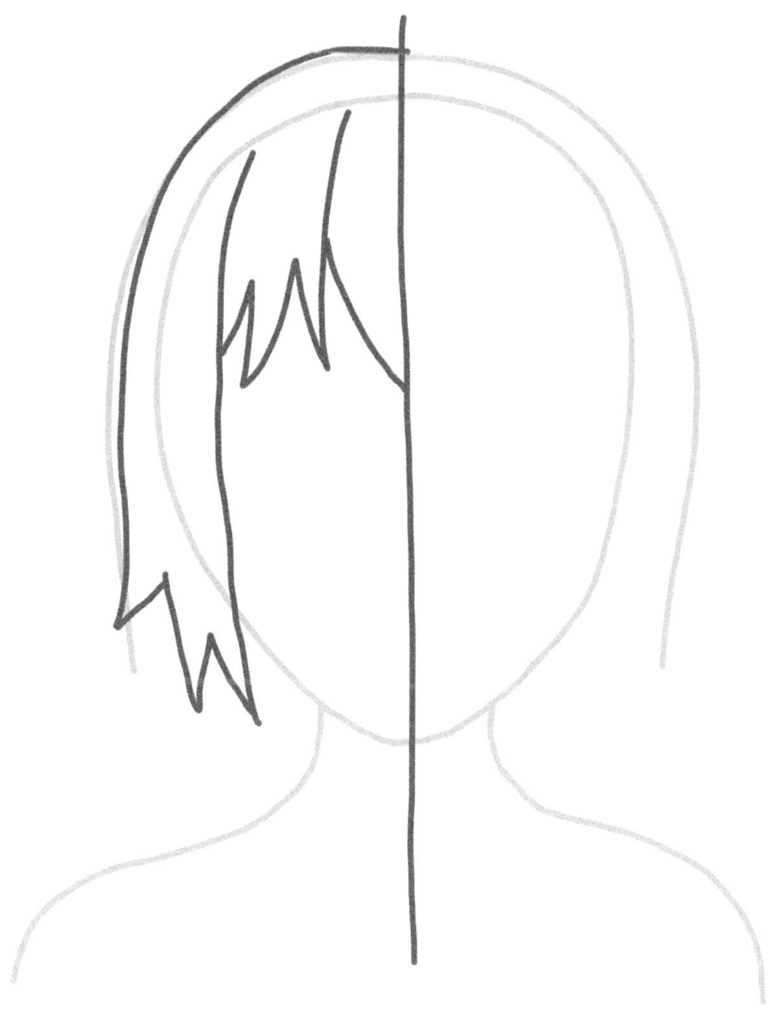

In this sketch you'll notice we've only completed half the hair. When we finish details we can draw the same mirrored hair on the other side of the head. This helps us to make sure we like the look before we draw the entire head of hair.

As demonstrated below, a mirror of the hair on the other side of the head will make your drawing complete.

There aren't any variations but in anime drawing most of the time the hair should be mirrored.

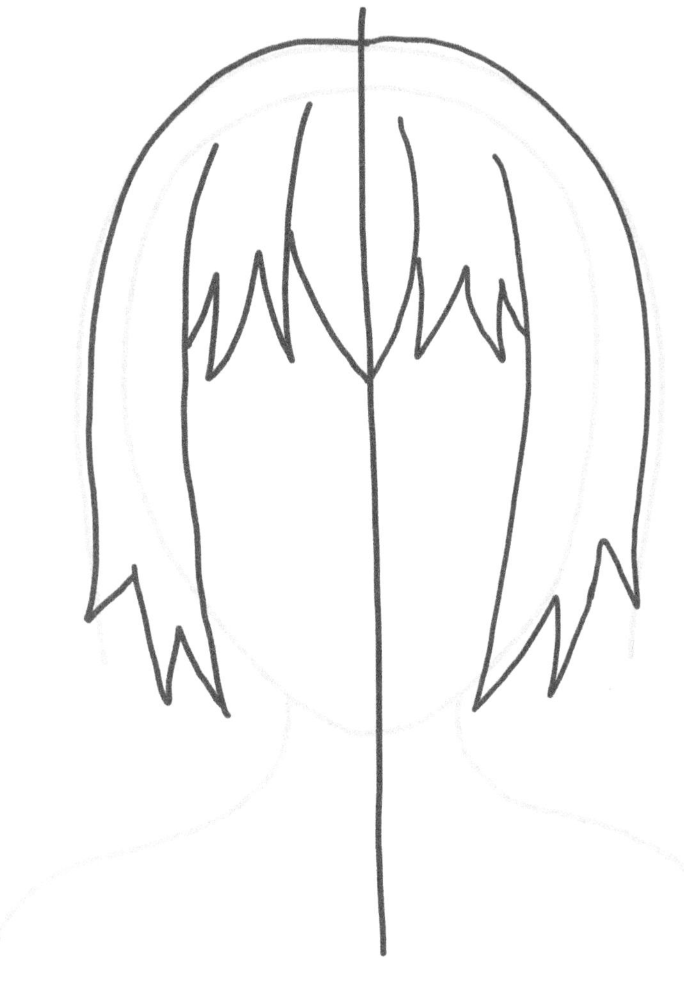

In the next pages we will cover how to do the details of the hair. You can either do the full head or just half. Practicing with just half will help you start drawing mirrored hair styles on your characters.

Practice Makes Perfect! Use the page below to practice drawing what you have learned so far.

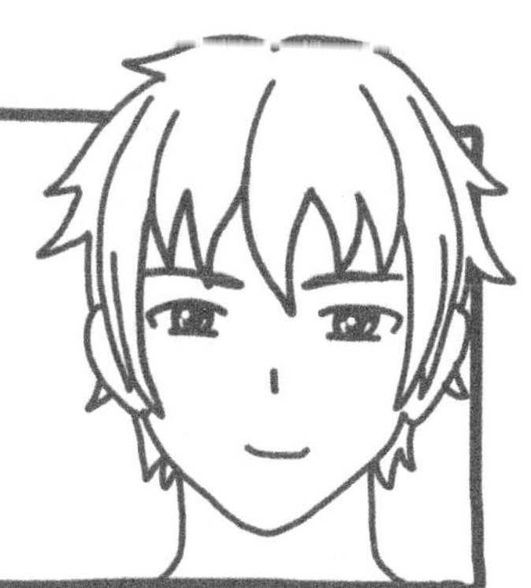

HAIR DETAILS

To draw the details in the hair, first start with shapes. Keep the shapes light so you can erase or draw over them.

Most hair styles have basic shapes in them to form the general look of the hair.

As demonstrated below look at the different shapes that outline the hair styles from the beginning of this section. Most shapes are basic ones including circles, rectangles, triangles, etc.

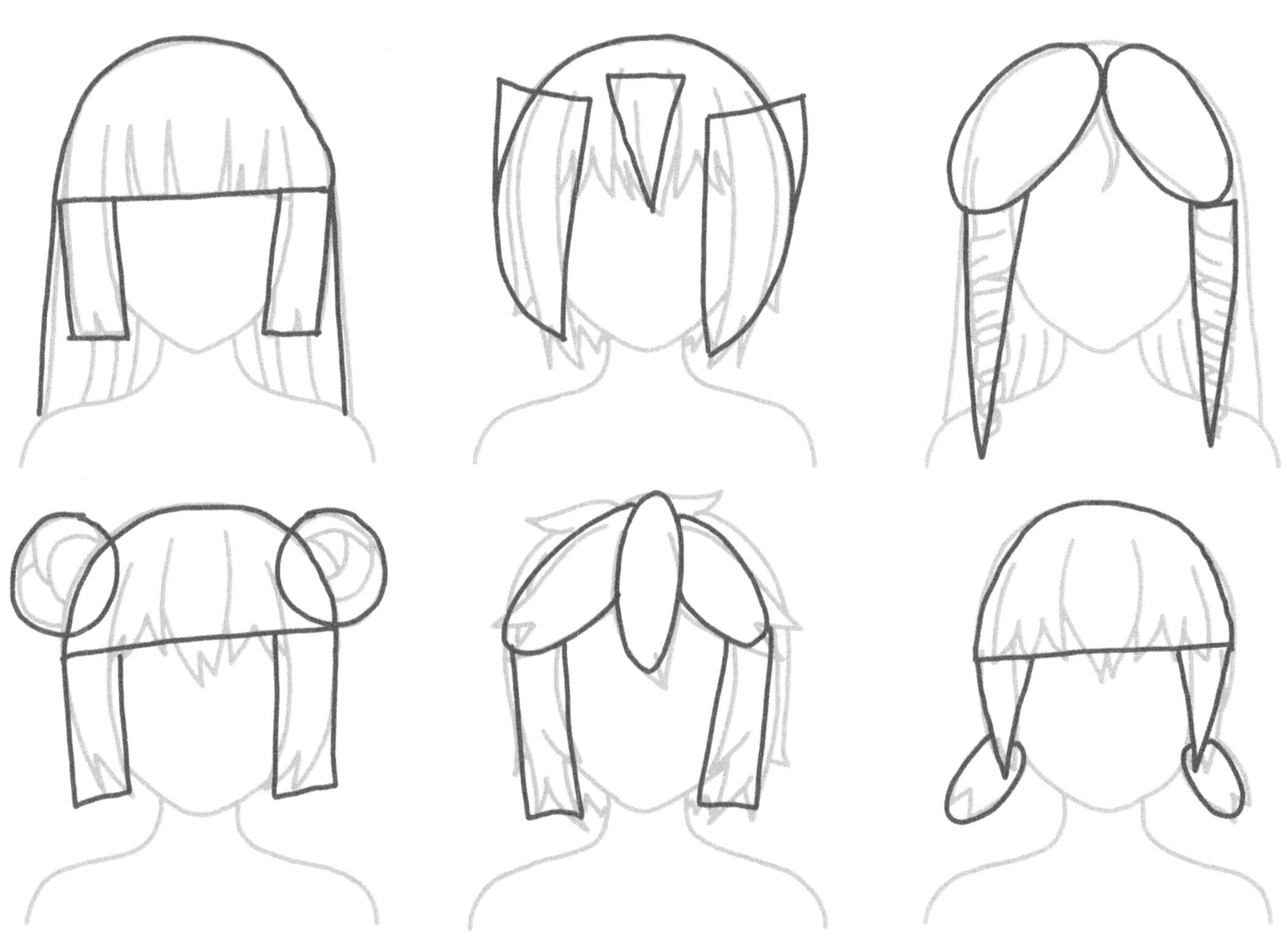

Practice drawing shapes over the hair styles below. There is no right or wrong way to do this.

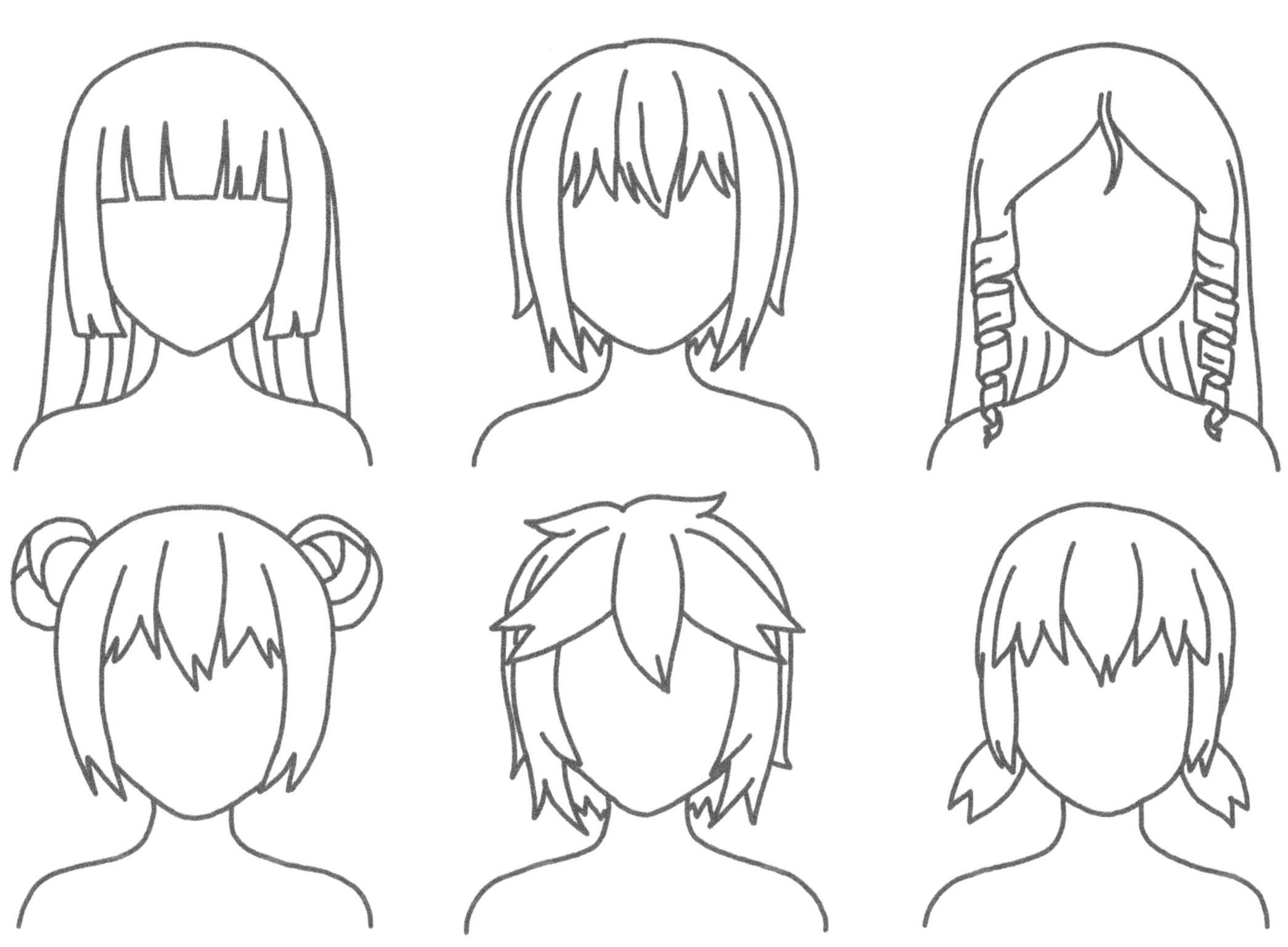

The main point of this exercise is to help you learn to spot shapes in hair styles.

As you move on you will draw the shapes first, but identifying them will give you ideas in your own hair styles.

If you get lost go back a page for ideas.

Practice Makes Perfect! Use the page below to practice drawing what you have learned so far.

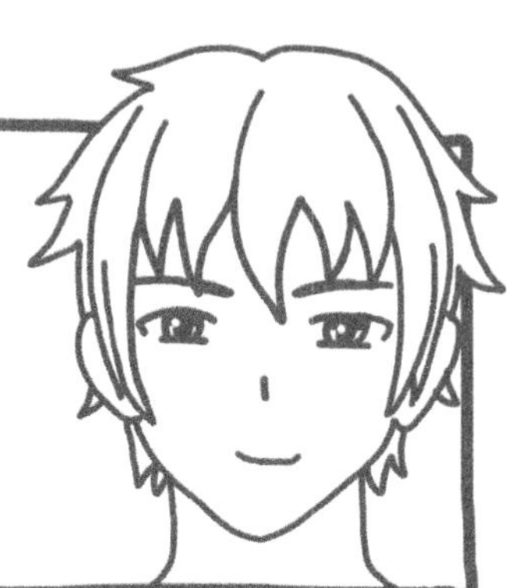

HAIR DETAILS

Let's start with one of the more simple hair styles. With this style it's just a few basic shapes to create a basic but great looking style. The style you see below has a few shapes that make it up.

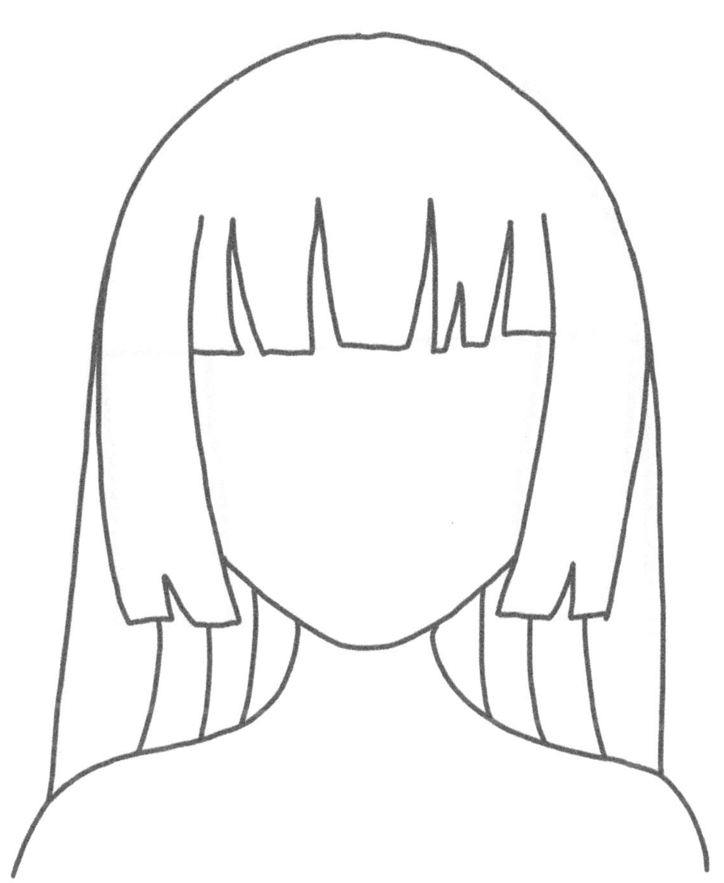

This is the finished look based on the shapes being filled in with details of the hair.

You may recall from the previous page that this hair style has mostly rectangles, one half circle on the top of the head and a couple of triangles where the hair drapes over the forehead.

Most hair styles use clean straight or curved lines throughout the head.

When drawing a hair style, draw the outline of the hair first, then add shapes throughout the outline.

Fill in details of the hair within the shapes. Make sure your shapes are drawn lightly so they can be erased later.

Connect any lines to finish the hair style up. Above is the hair style we have been working on with just the basic lines.

Practice using the head below to draw a hair style. Use the following steps:

1. Draw an outline of the hair around the head.

2. Draw shapes inside the outline where you want the details to go.

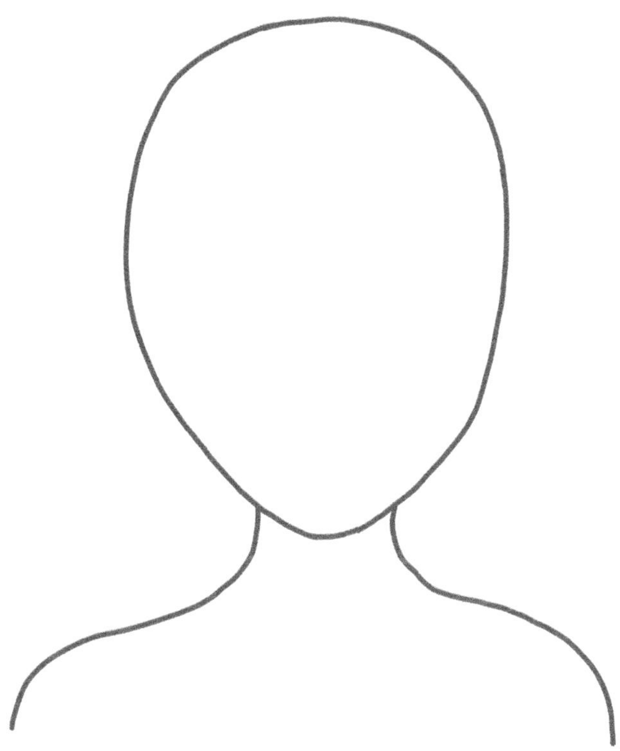

3. Draw lines inside the shapes that will represent the direction the hair will flow.

4. Last finish by connecting the lines and erasing any trace of the shapes.

Practice Makes Perfect! Use the page below to practice drawing what you have learned so far.

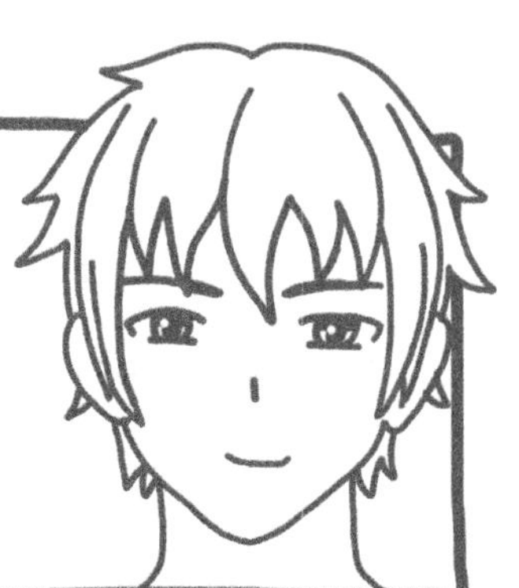

Using the examples below, practice drawing your own heads and hair.

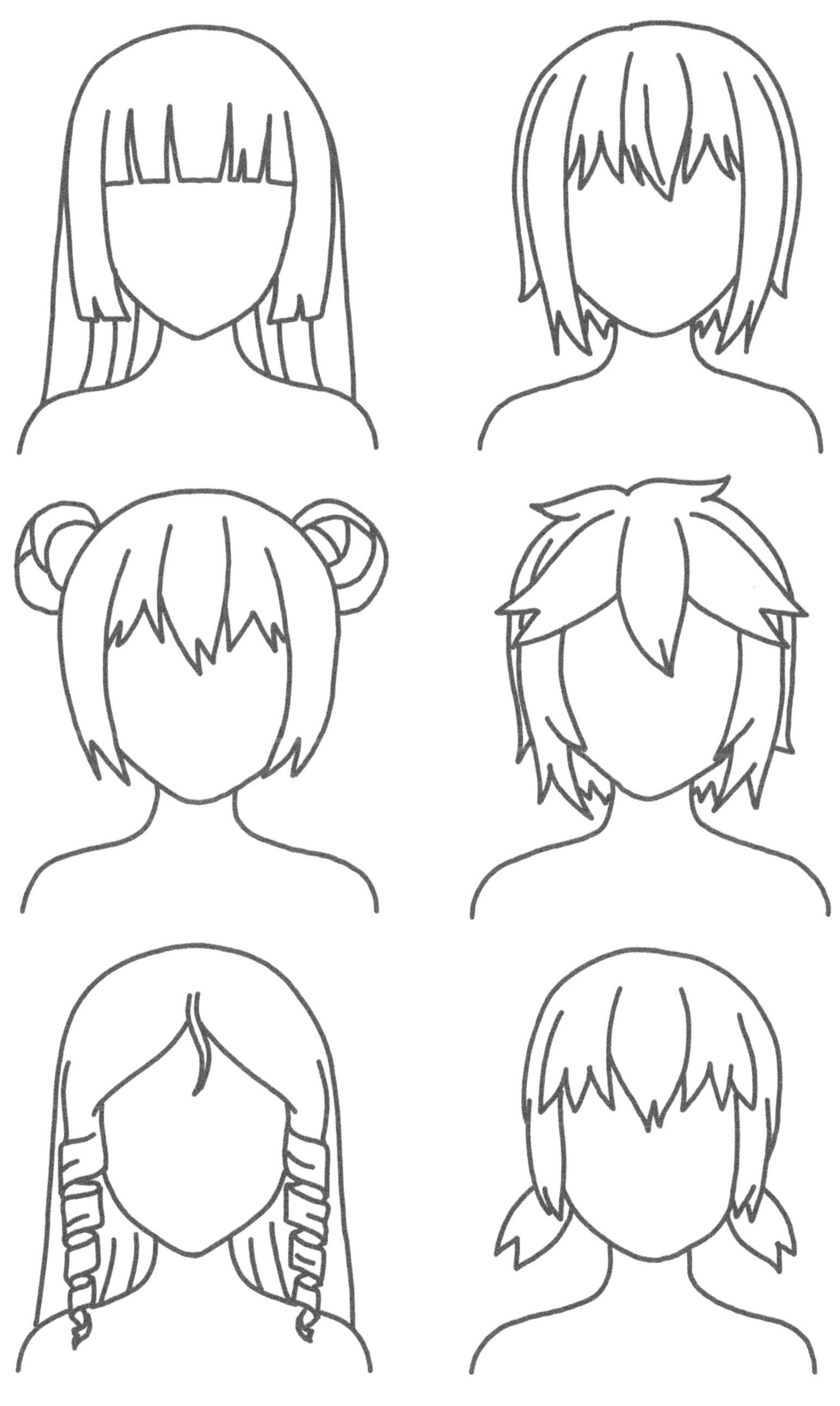

CONCLUSION

Drawing hair is by far one of the more difficult anime characteristics to master. As with all drawing the only way to get better at it, is to practice.

As you get better at drawing hair, try using different hair styles you find to experiment and try on your own.

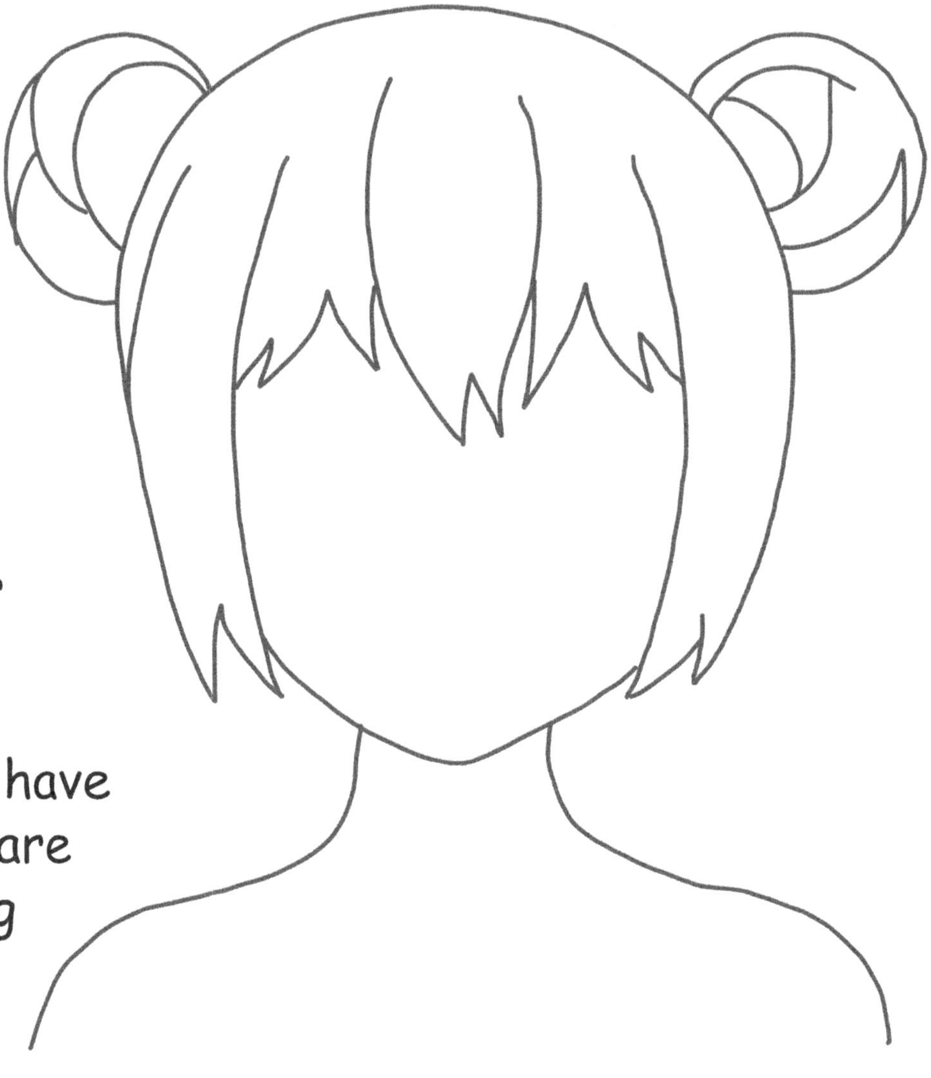

The styles you have learned so far are for the drawing steps only in anime hair for girls.

There are additional steps like shading and color that will be covered in another book.

For now practice the basics!

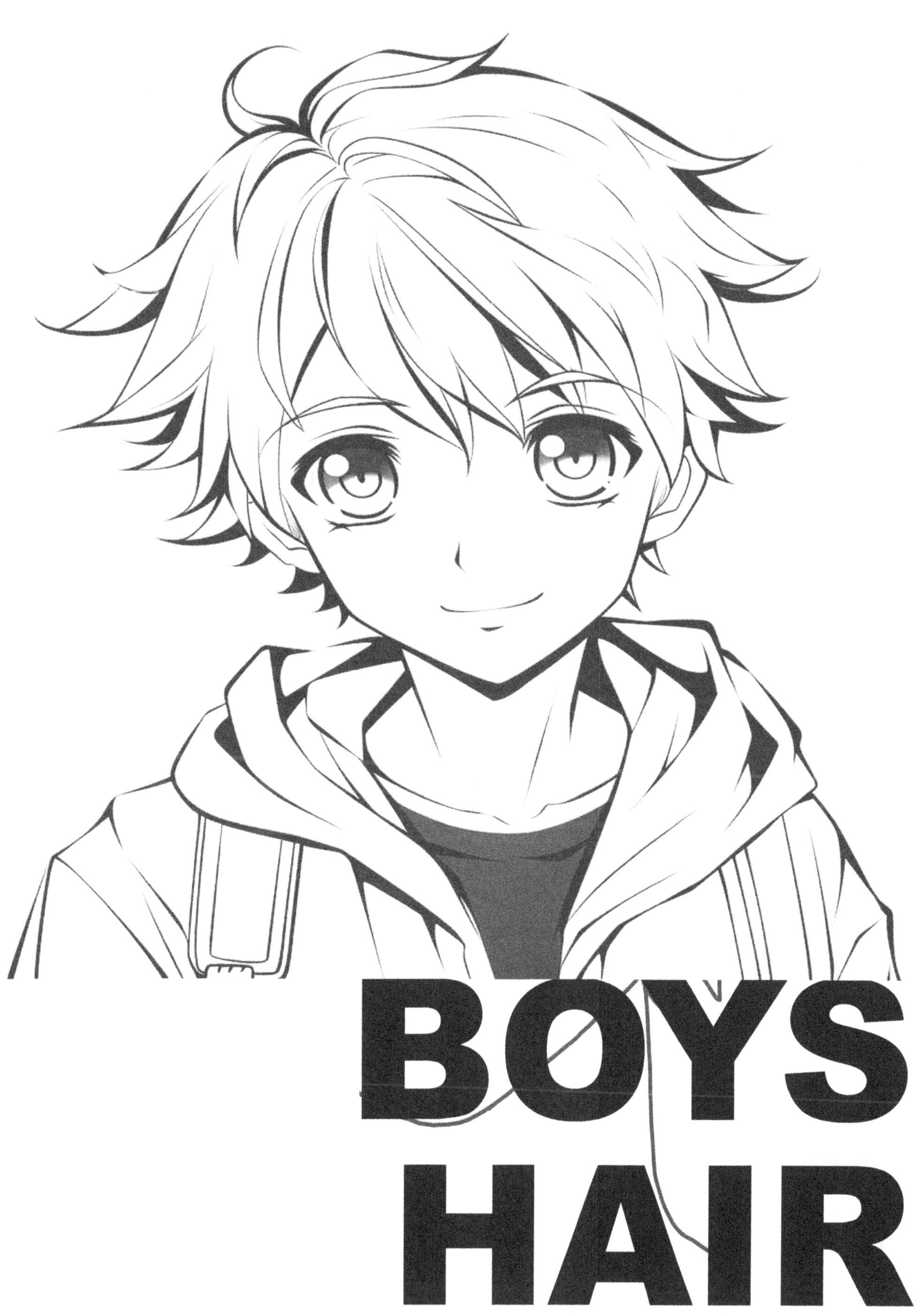
BOYS
HAIR

BOYS HAIR

Boys hair styles are just as varying and difficult to draw as girls styles. As you can see below there are just as many options.

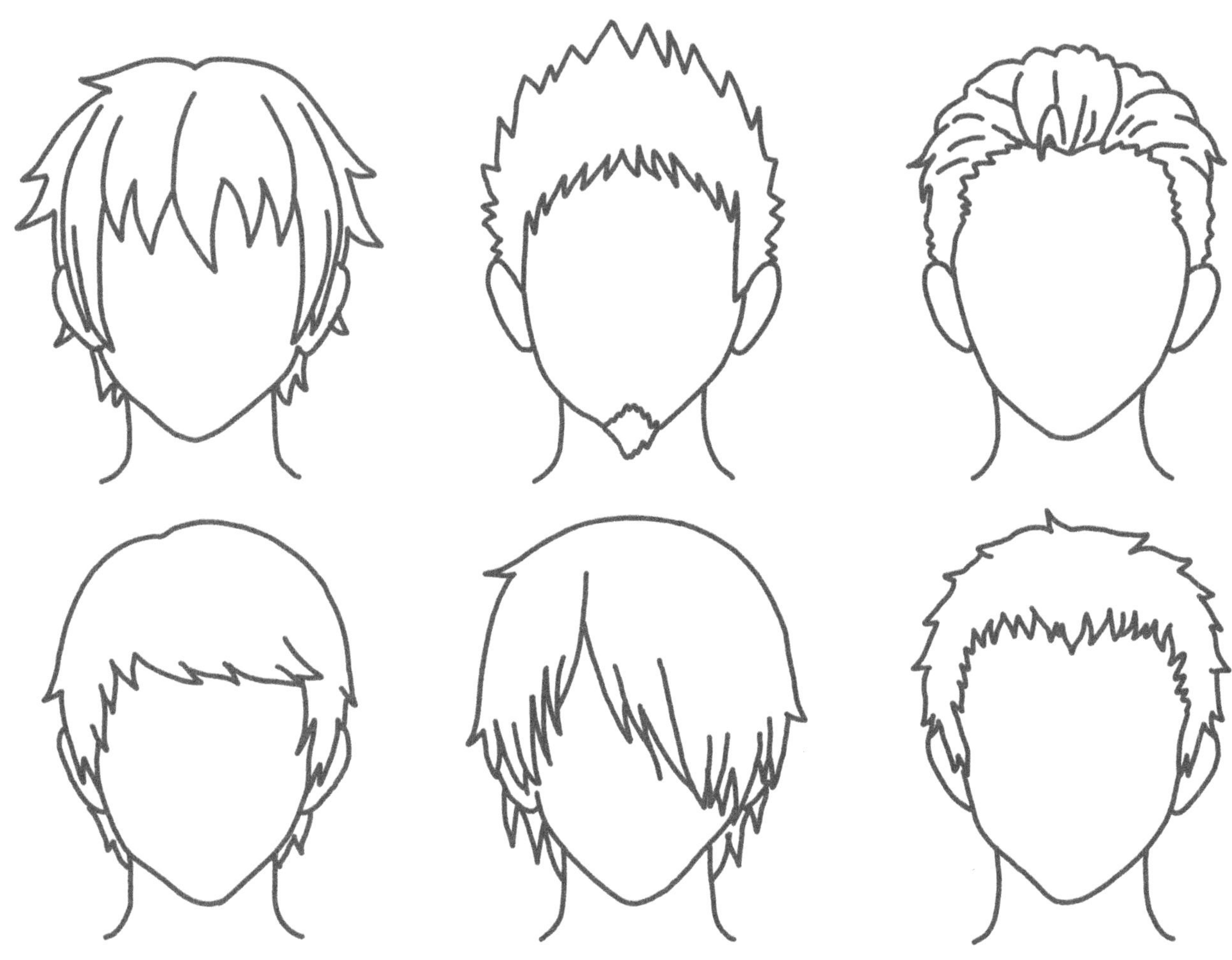

Additionally there is actually an added level of complexity when drawing boys hair.

This is because of ears and chins being more visible on boys than girls.

If the symmetry is not correct on the hair, the face will look wrong.

Hair generally follows the contour of the face just the same as for girls. There are a couple of differences to consider.

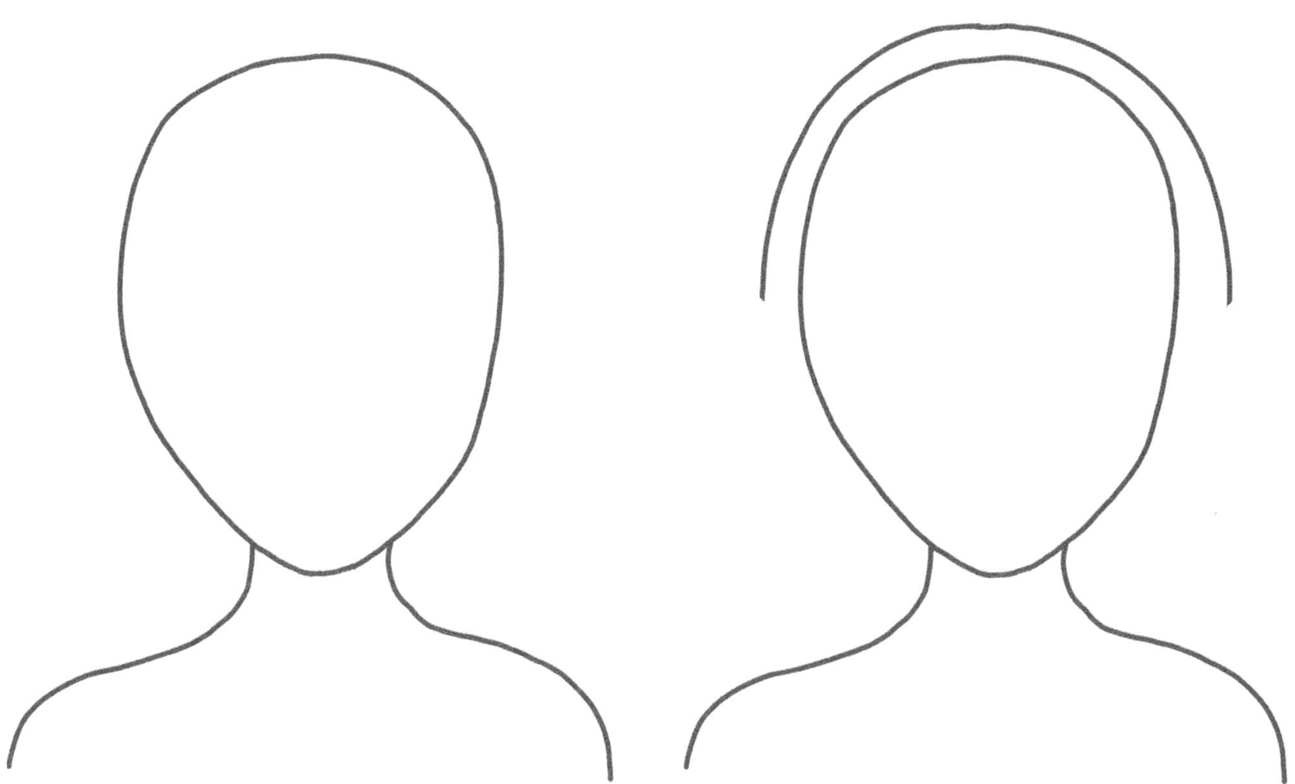

For boys the hair doesn't drop usually all the way to the shoulders. Instead the outline should stop about mid-way down the sides of the head.

This is also where you start the ears.

Pro-Tip: Boys hair although more difficult can usually be fixed by adding more jagged pieces. Boys = Jagged, Girls = Flowing.

Boys hair also uses shapes to determine the outline of the hair. The easy part though is that boys hair uses mainly one shape.

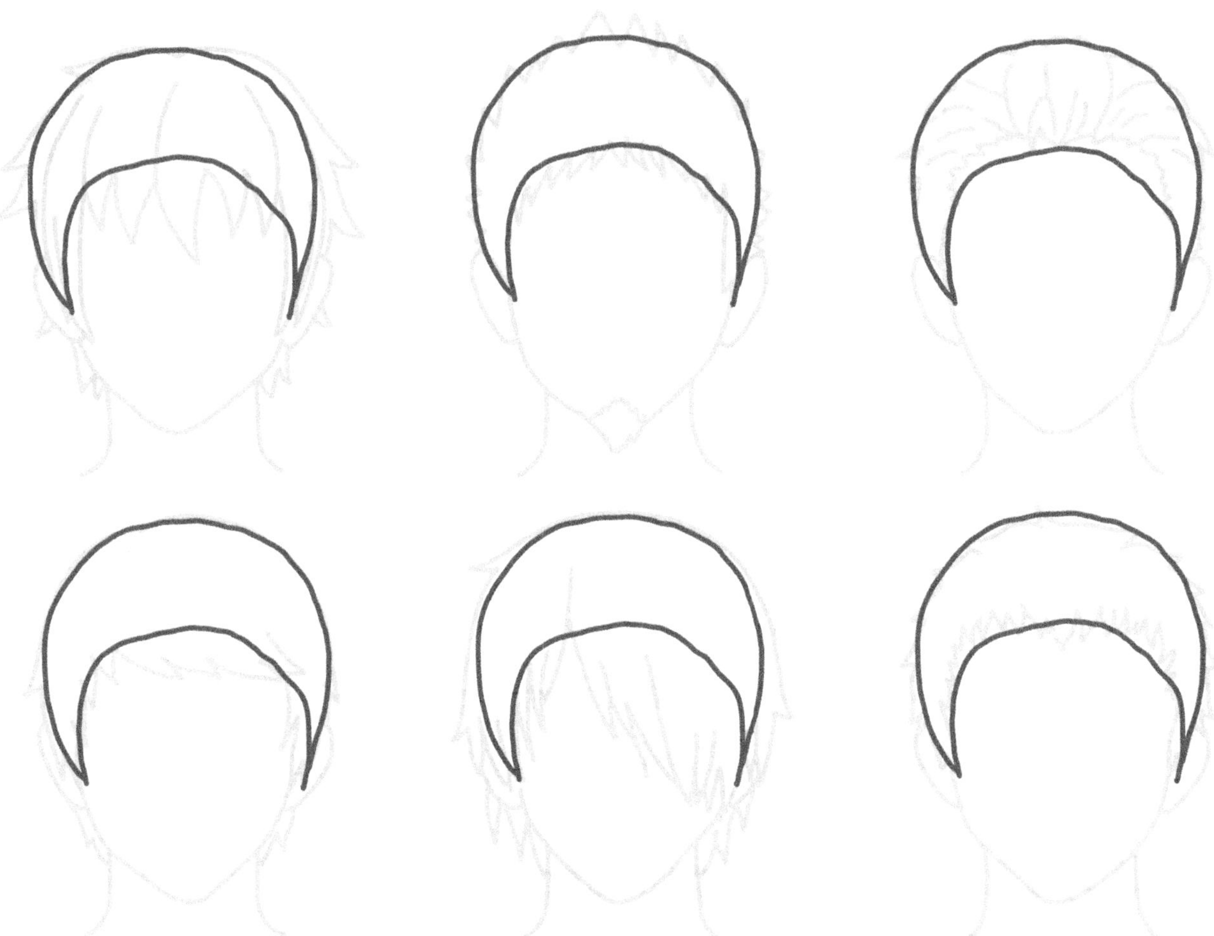

As you can see from the above heads, the main shape is a half moon shape on it's side. This general shape will be the base that you will work off of when drawing boys hair.

There will be some variations but this shape should give the main size of the boys hair.

Practice Makes Perfect! Use the page below to practice drawing what you have learned so far.

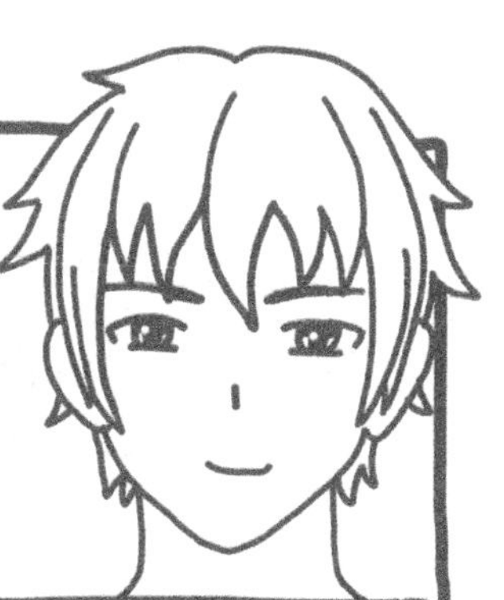

After you draw the half moon shape you can add more details to the hair. If you look at the main shapes of a boys hair is there anything you notice?

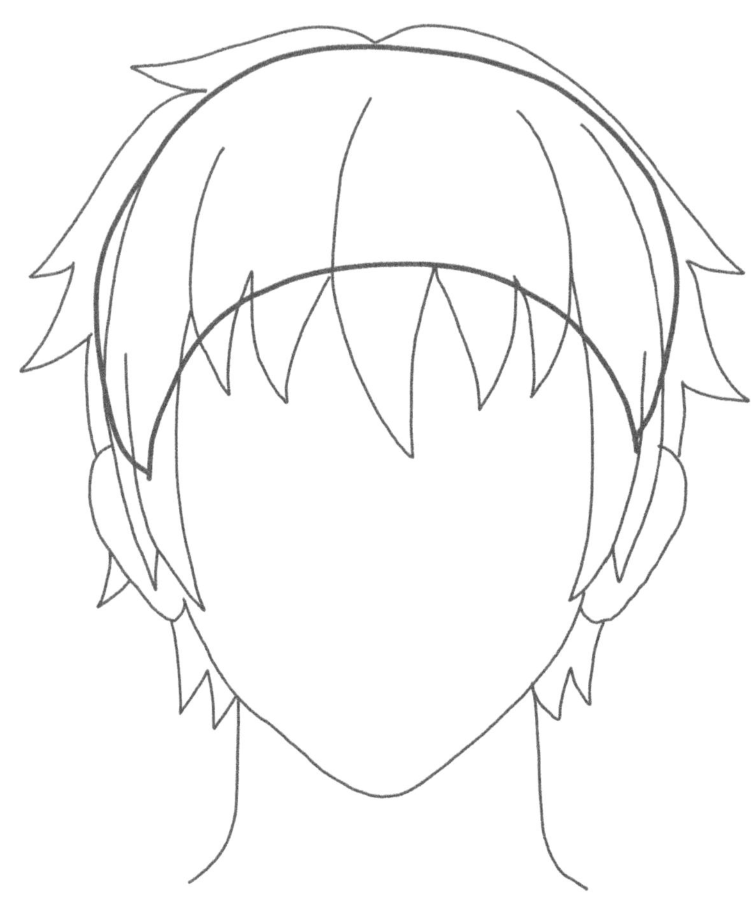

You probably notice that all the hair chunks point down. If you look closer they also look like a bunch of shark fins, or knife blades. Imagine drawing those as you practice drawing hair.

Pro-Tip: Drawing hair does not have to be hard. Move your pen back and forth in the same area and you'll find it's actually easy.

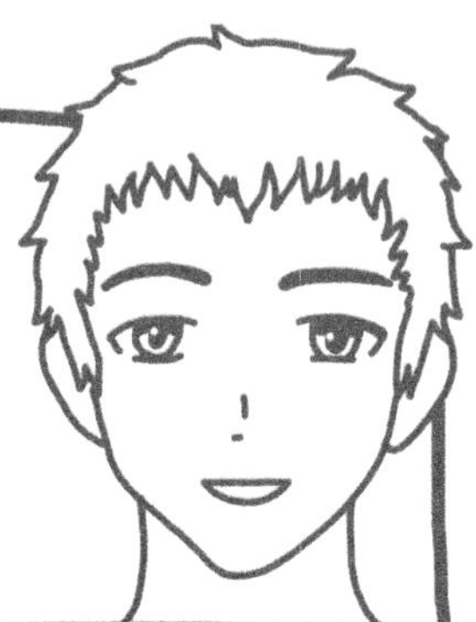

Practice drawing hair on the figure below by using the following steps:

1. Draw an outline of the hair to half way down the side of the head.

2. Draw a half moon shape along the outline and through the forehead.

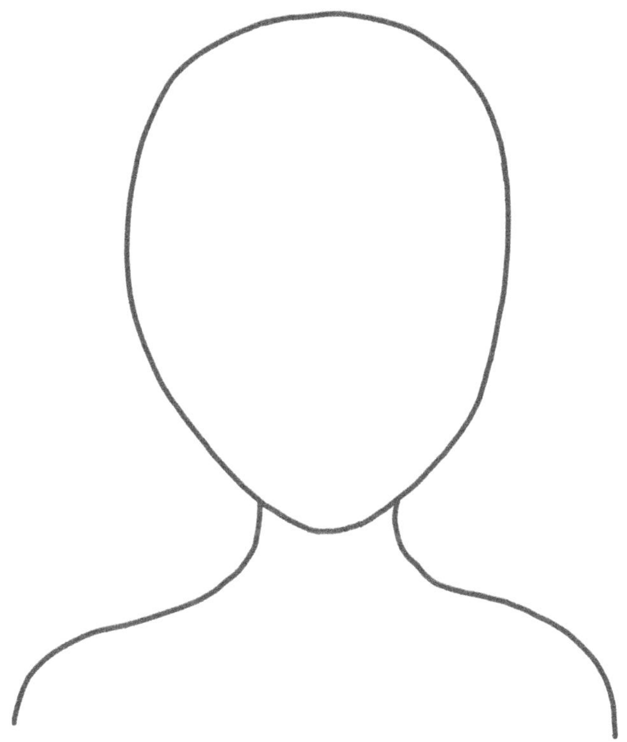

3. Draw the shapes of fins or knife blades pointing down from the half-moon shape on the head.

4. Erase any extra lines in your hair that do not go along with the details that should be there.

Practice Makes Perfect! Use the page below to practice drawing what you have learned so far.

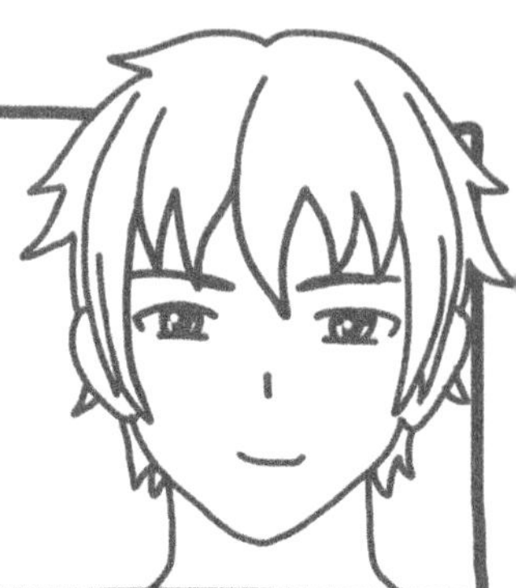

Practice on your own drawing the heads below. Try switching features up to get better at creating your own.

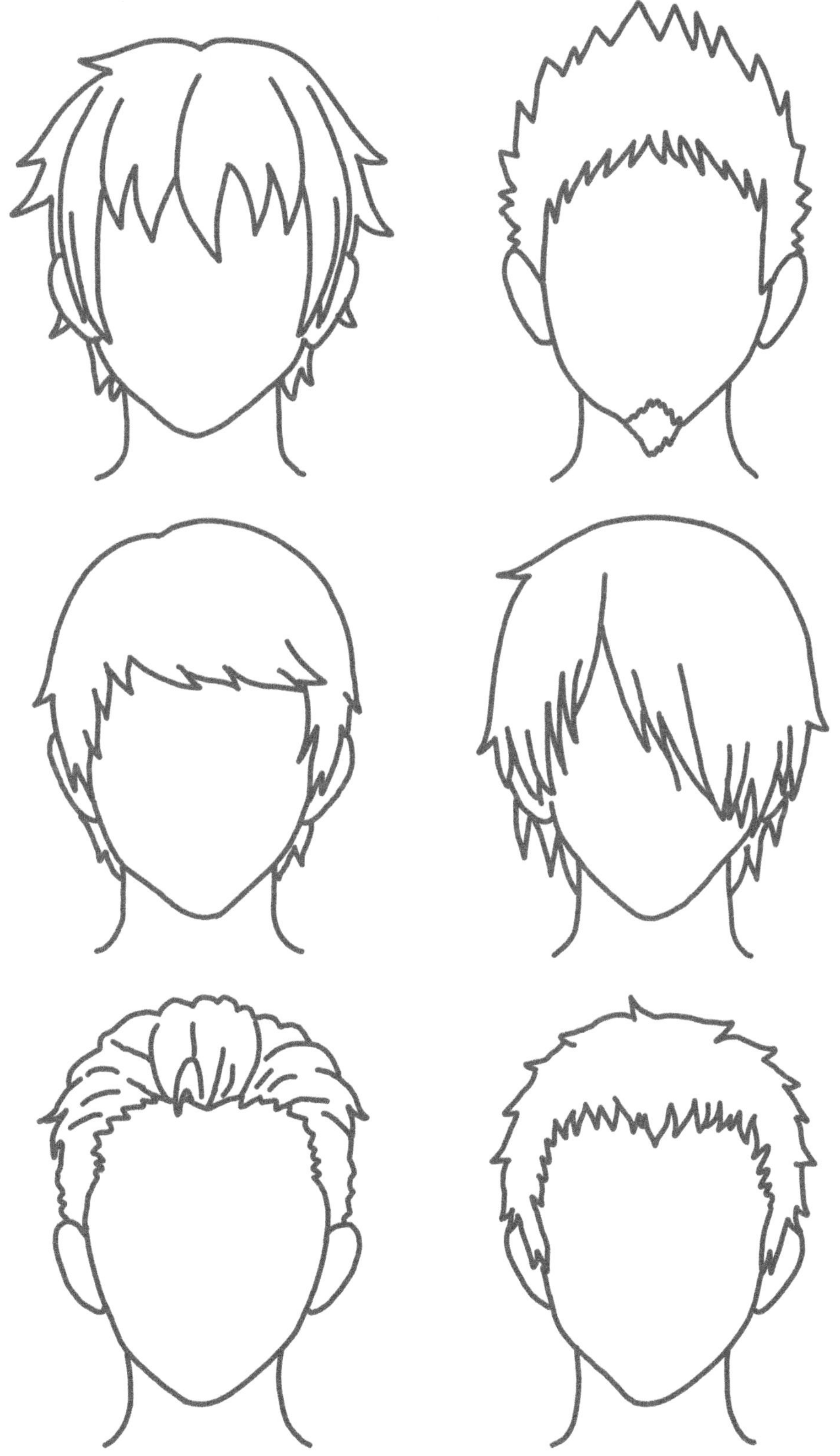

CONCLUSION

Like drawing girls hair, boys hair takes practice and patience as you learn how to do it correctly. There are some tricks that will help you get better at it that we have added to this chapter. In the end however nothing will help you more than practice.

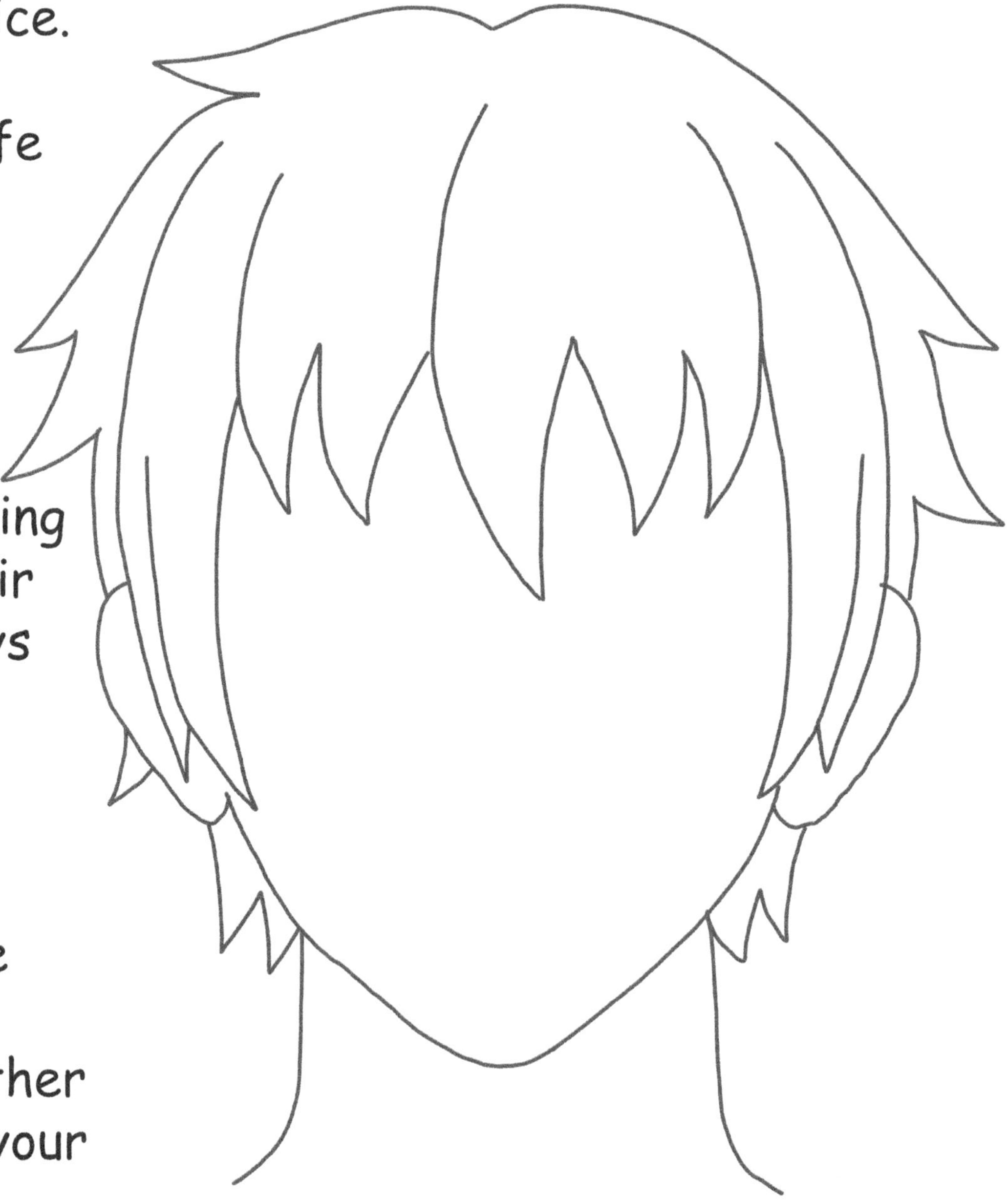

Use real-life examples or even people you know as models while learning to draw hair onboth boys and girls.

As you continue to practice drawing hair and other features, your anime characters will begin to look amazing!

Use this page to practice what you have learned.

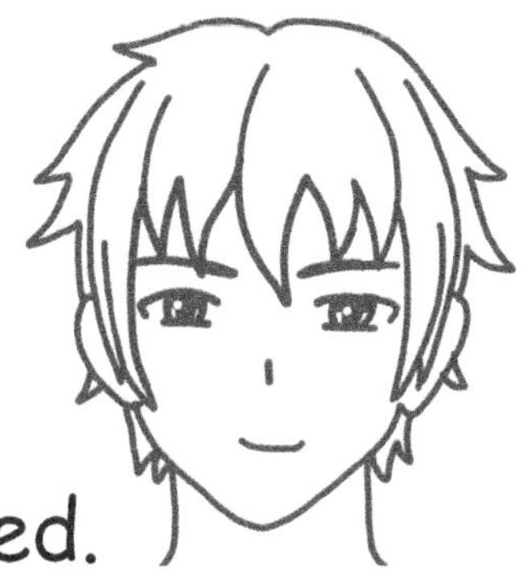

Use this page to practice what you've learned.

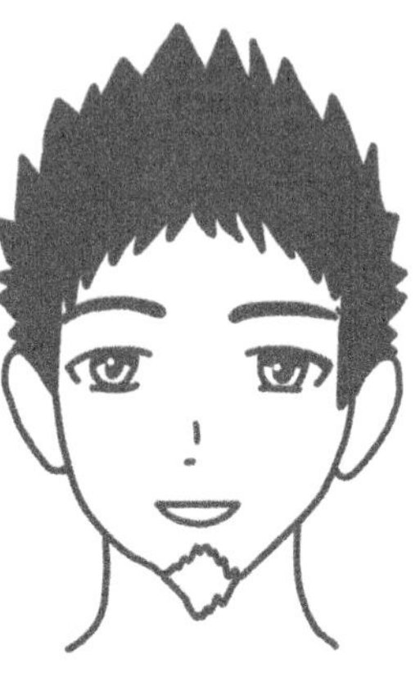

Use this page to practice what you've learned.

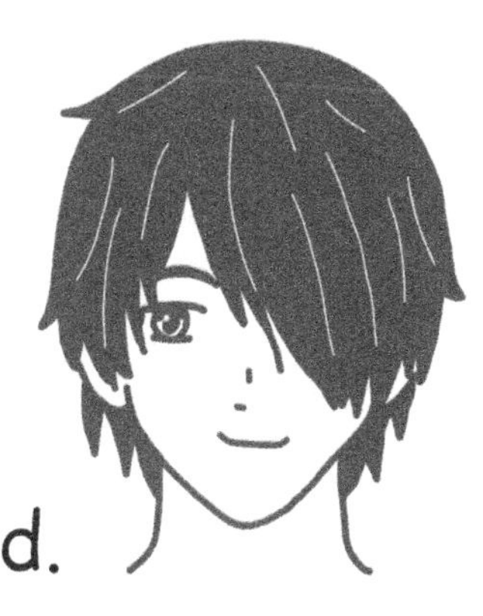

Use this page to practice what you've learned.

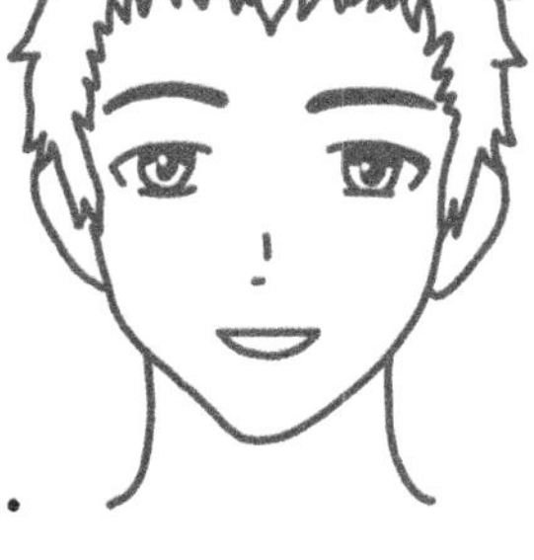

Use this page to practice what you have learned.

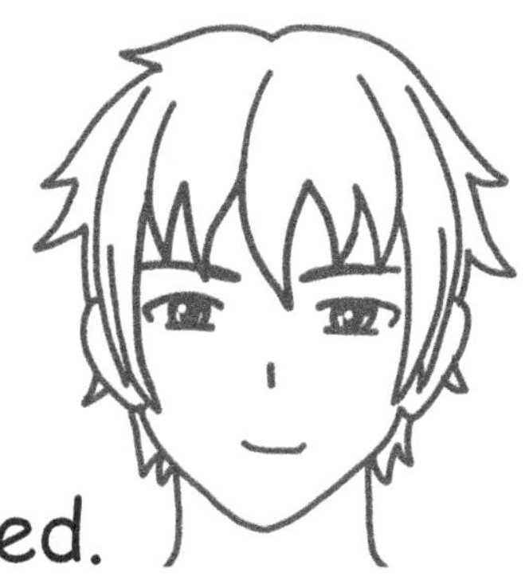

Use this page to practice what you've learned.

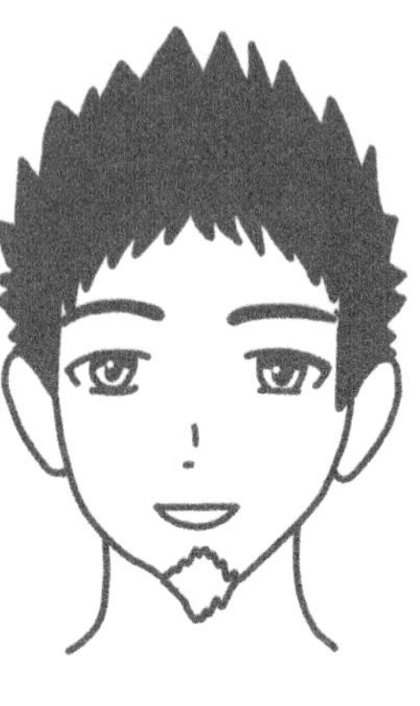

Use this page to practice what you've learned.

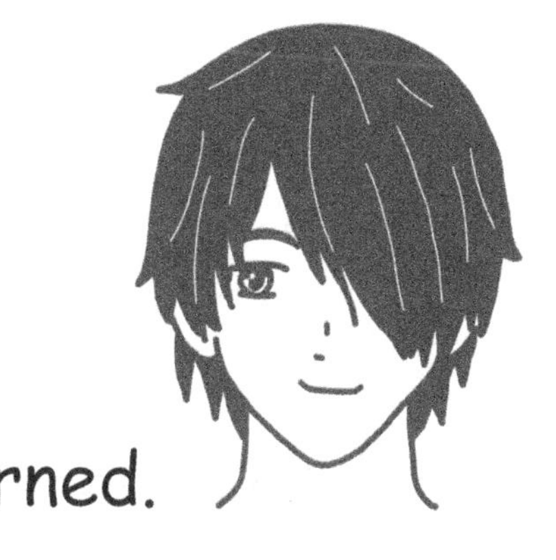

Use this page to practice what you've learned.

Use this page to practice what you have learned.

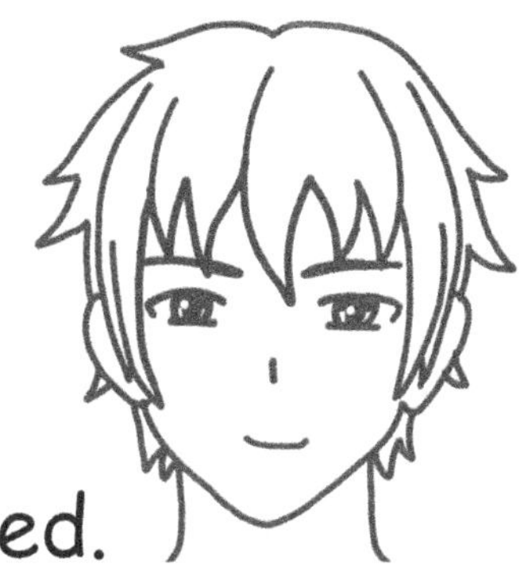

Use this page to practice what you've learned.

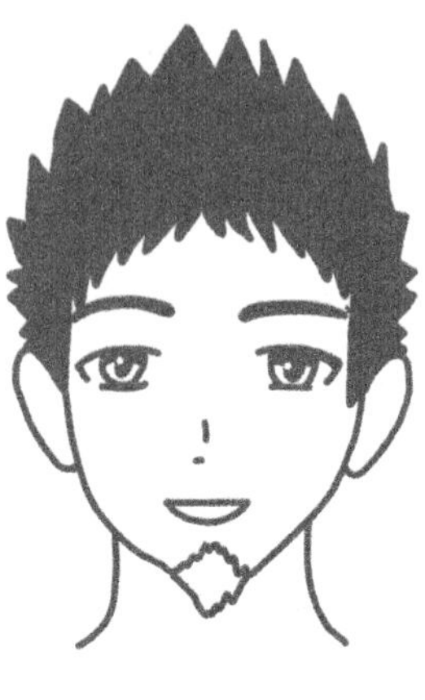

Use this page to practice what you've learned.

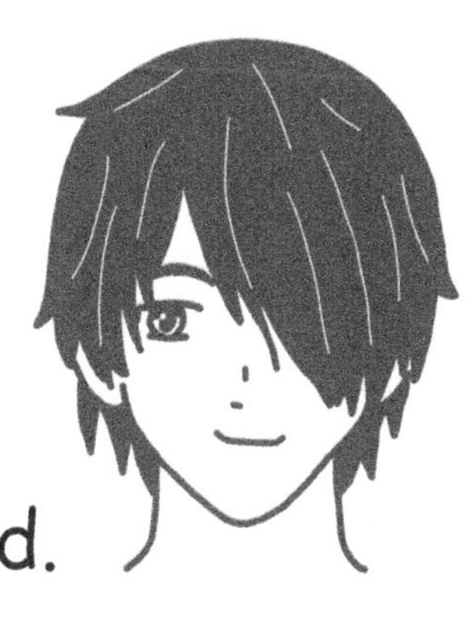

Use this page to practice what you've learned.

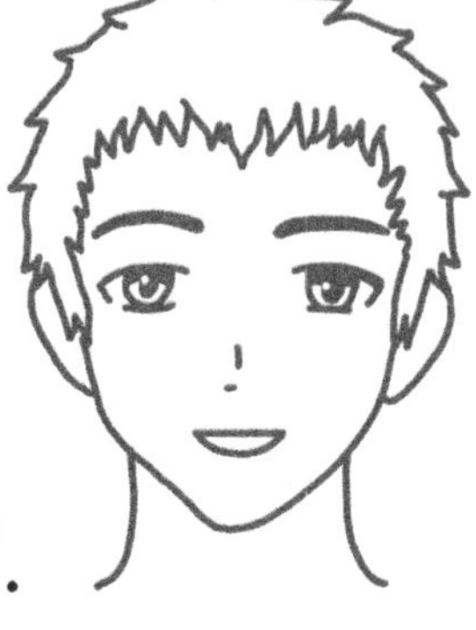

Use this page to practice what you have learned.

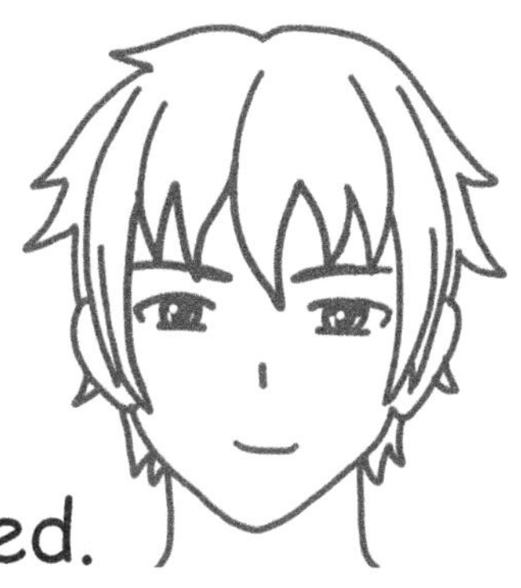

Use this page to practice what you've learned.

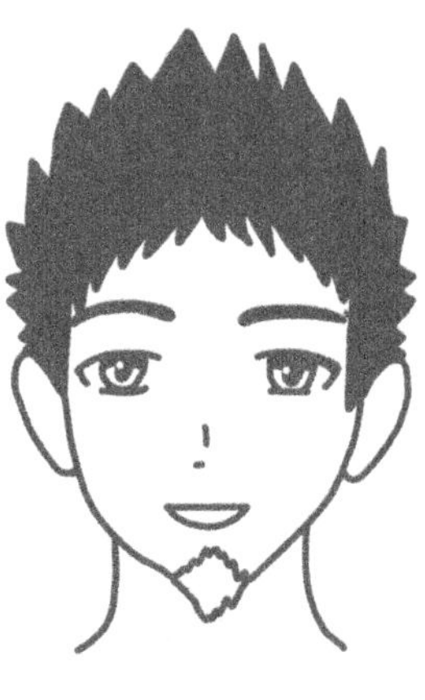

Use this page to practice what you've learned.

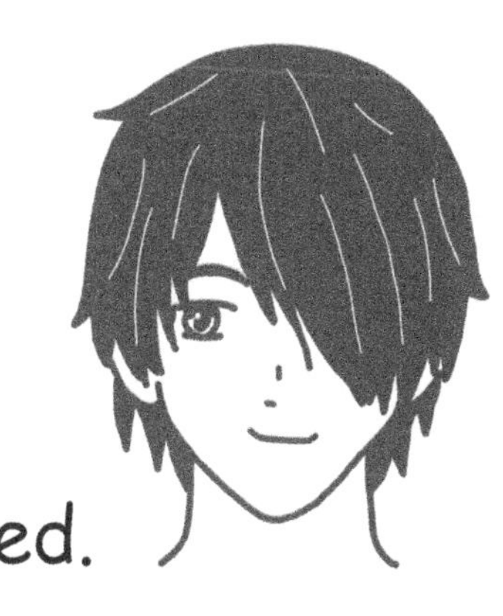

Use this page to practice what you've learned.

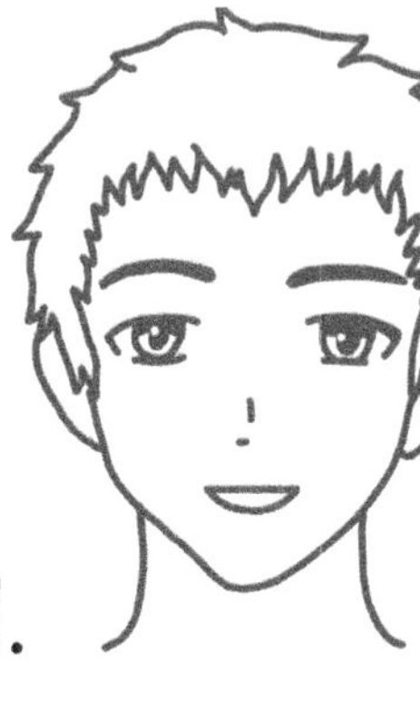

Use this page to practice what you have learned.

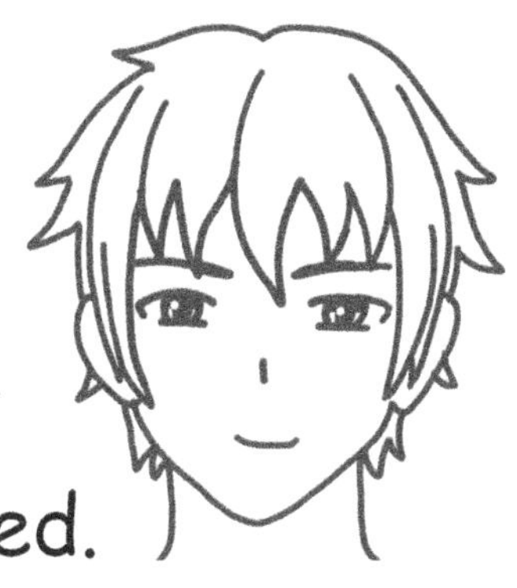

Use this page to practice what you've learned.

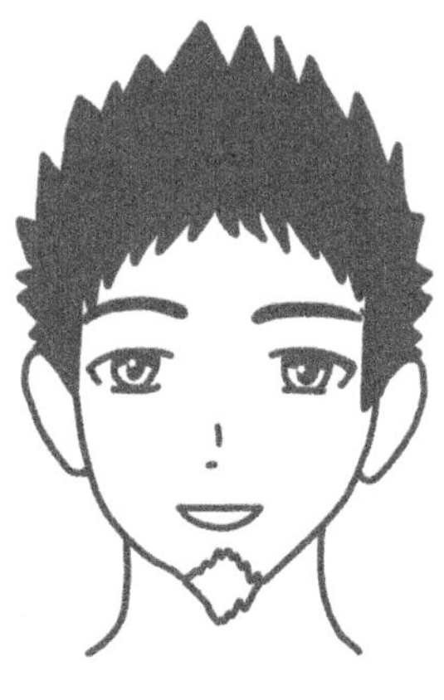

Use this page to practice what you've learned.

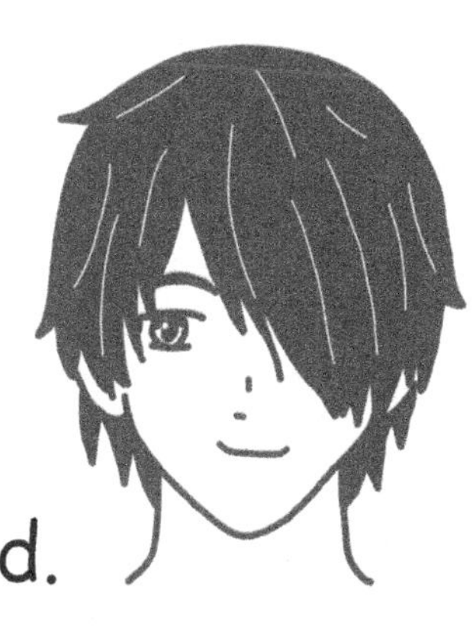

Use this page to practice what you've learned.

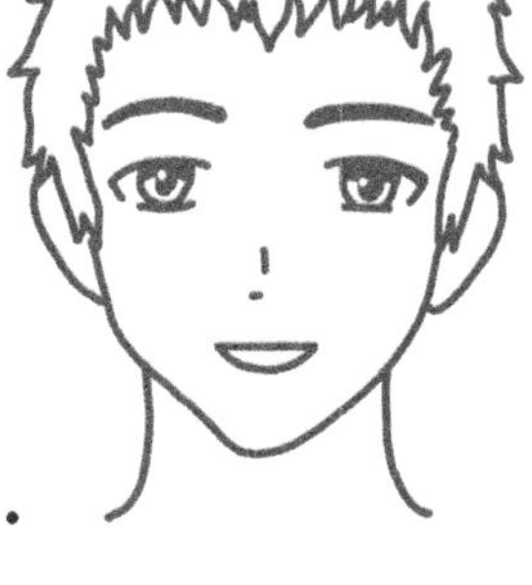

Use this page to practice what you have learned.

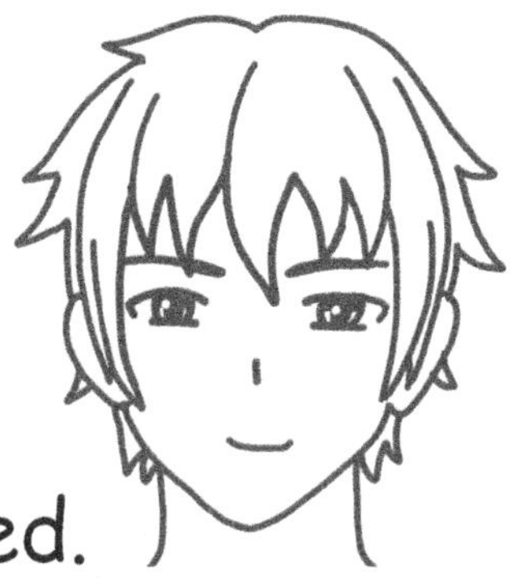

Use this page to practice what you've learned.

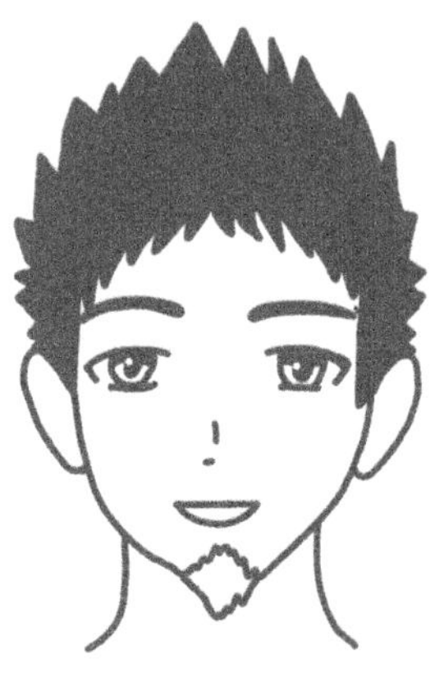

Use this page to practice what you've learned.

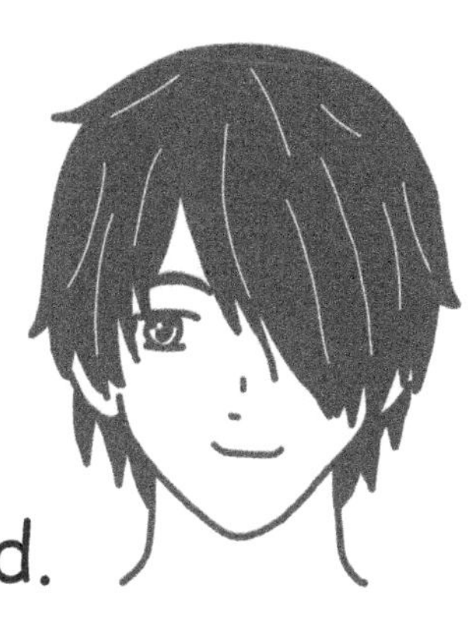

Use this page to practice what you've learned.

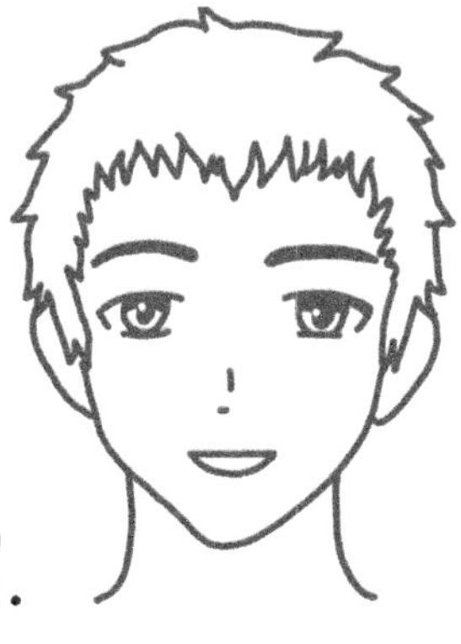

Use this page to practice what you have learned.

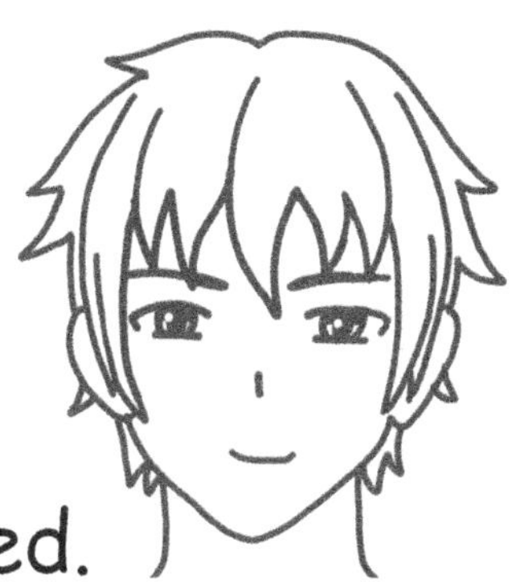

Made in the USA
Coppell, TX
17 November 2023

24344463R00063